REALM OF THE INCAS

MAX MILLIGAN

FOREWORD BY JOHN HEMMING

Idlewild Publishers

For four people to whom I owe much more than this:
Robert Randall, Wendy Weeks, Barry Walker and
Max Gunther, who chose to take me in and teach me,
year after year after year.

And to my family, who never had much choice.

Revised edition published in 2003 by
IDLEWILD (*Publishers*),
Row Court, Laverton,
Bath, Somerset,
BA2 7RA

First published in 2001 by
HarperCollins*Publishers*

Photographs and text © 2003 Max Milligan
Foreword © 2003 John Hemming

Max Milligan hereby asserts his moral right to
be identified as the author of this Work.

A CIP catalogue record for this book is available
from the British Library.

ISBN: 0-9545876-0-X

Designed and typeset by Isambard Thomas
Colour origination by Colourscan, Singapore
Printed and bound by Imago, Singapore

FRONT COVER Ukukus, 'bear-men' messengers
between the living and the dead, raise their masks
briefly, before carrying sacred ice back down to the
sanctuary of Qollur Rit'i.

BACK COVER A giant tree fern above a cloud forest
trail in Vilcabamba.

PAGES 2–3 (left to right) Ukuku pilgrims await the
first rays of sun on a sacred glacier; a father carries
his injured son through the Vilcabamba highlands;
Lake Pacucha shines in stormy light from the
hilltop Sondor fortress; dawn breaks through
humid rainforest air on the Tambopata river.

THIS PAGE Awaiting a fresh trout breakfast, an old
man soaks up the sun in a cantina kitchen.

FOREWORD

In November 1532 Francisco Pizarro made a reckless decision: he would leave the coast of Peru and march inland to meet the Inca Atahualpa. As they left the tenuous security of a maritime escape route, Pizarro and his 168 men had their first impression of the verticality of the Andes and realized the extent to which the Incas were mountain people. Their horses had difficulty climbing the steep trails, and the conquistadors were frightened by the ravines and passes in which they could easily have been trapped.

A year later, after the tiny band of invaders had seized Atahualpa, melted down his huge ransom of gold and silver, broken their promise to release him, and then executed the Inca, they were free to march south to the imperial capital, Cuzco. The 685-mile (1,100km) journey along paved Inca highways showed more of the jagged mountain terrain of central Peru. Pizarro's men were forever plunging down precipitous slopes, coaxing their horses over rope suspension bridges spanning great gorges, or toiling up slopes that seemed to soar into the clouds. No one understood that the earth's atmosphere thins with altitude, but the Spaniards became aware that the indigenous Peruvians were better adapted to exertion in the high Andes – in battle, they themselves were heavily dependent on their horses.

The verticality of Peru is a strong theme of Max Milligan's book. His magnificent photographs sweep from the snows and glaciers of the Vilcanota mountains, down to the treeless *puna* of high-altitude savanna, to the fertile valleys of the Incas' heartlands, and then down to the tropical rainforests of the Amazon thousands of feet below. His pictures of Andean Indians also show

how they have evolved to live at high altitude. Their handsome coppery skins and the children's apple-red cheeks are signs of this adaption, just as their physiognomy belies their race's origins in the high plateaus of central Asia.

After the conquest of Peru was complete, the Spaniards held inquiries to learn more about Inca administration and systems of tribute. They discovered, to their surprise, that the Inca state had a vertical organization. Communities in the highlands ran down into the *yungas*, or lowland valleys, of the Amazon forests. This meant that groups in the mountains had workers in satellite outposts far below, so that they could be supplied with coca, manioc and all the tropical fruits, medicinal plants and exotic birds and animals. This vertical symmetry is true of the modern Peruvian Región Inka, the local authority that embraces the Inca lands around Cuzco and the edge of the Amazon forests to the east. This is the exciting region covered by Milligan's book. He shows the extraordinary circular terraces of Moray, sunk into the altiplano not far from Cuzco, which were evidently for agricultural experiment – to reproduce in miniature the altitudinal zones of the empire's farming habitats.

The book also shows the wonders of Cuzco, to me one of the world's most beautiful cities, and of the nearby Sacred Valley, the favourite retreat of the Inca rulers. The line of Inca ruins goes from Pisaq to Ollantaytambo and on to the incomparable Machu Picchu. This holy 'lost city' was in a sense a pilgrimage goal for the Incas, just as it is now for hikers along the Inca Trail, and for every visitor to Peru. No one is disappointed by Machu Picchu. But Milligan also shows the southwestern part of the Región Inka, the lands of the upper Apurimac where life continues in its traditional rhythm and almost no visitors penetrate.

Alongside its mountain scenery, luxuriant forests, virtuoso Inca stonemasonry and exuberant baroque architecture, Peru's great attraction is its people. It is the Quechua and Aymara Indians, the creoles of Spanish descent, and the mestizos proud enough to combine the best of both races, that give Peru its individuality. This mix emerges throughout the pictures in this book, and Milligan even manages to capture the different characters of the country's human diversity.

A sixteenth-century Spaniard, Miguel Agia, summed up the contrast between the conquerors and their subjects: 'The Spaniard and Indian are diametrically opposed. The Indian is by nature without greed and the Spaniard is extremely greedy, the Indian phlegmatic and the Spaniard excitable, the Indian humble and the Spaniard arrogant, the Indian deliberate in all he does and the Spaniard quick in all he wants, the one liking to order and the other hating to serve.' The excesses of the European masters have been curbed in modern Peru, but the indigenous character has not changed greatly. Indians remain conservative, stoical, uninterested in politics but loyal to family and community, and highly spiritual. These attitudes can be seen in the illustrations in this book.

The Runa, the regimented peasantry of the Inca empire, lost heavily in the change of masters after the conquest. The paternalistic organization of the Incas was destroyed for ever, along with the great stores of foods, provision for emergencies, even the roads, irrigation channels and agricultural terracing. In their place came oppression by greedy *encomenderos*, officials and priests, all of whom demanded massive tribute in kind and forced labour by men and women. The cruelty increased when one of the world's greatest silver mines was discovered at Potosí in Bolivia and the mercury to extract the precious metal came from noxious mines at Huancavelíca in Peru. Tens of thousands of Indians toiled and died in these 'mouths of hell'.

The elaborate Inca religion was, of course, replaced by Christianity. Catholic priests made a determined (but only partly successful) effort to smash shrines and totems and to 'extirpate idolatry'. But the Church has also served as the solace and often the main protector of the indigenous Peruvians. A visitor has only to see the fervour of devotion and the delight in saints' days and processions, that take place in towns and villages on every day of the year, to appreciate how much the Indians love their churches. That piety (alongside relics of pre-conquest and folk beliefs) is vividly portrayed in many pictures in Max Milligan's fine anthology. It tells people much about Peru, and will be a dazzling reminder should they visit.

John Hemming
London, May 2001

INTRODUCTION

Everything in Peru, in some ways seems to be a peak   the colours there are almost unbelievable   it was so beautiful one was often left speechless and by night one thought, maybe it wasn't real – maybe it was a dream.
GEORGIA O'KEEFFE IN A LETTER TO HER FRIEND ANITA POLLITZER

In the variety of its charms and the power of its spell, I know of no place in the world which can compare with it.
HIRAM BINGHAM *Lost City of the Incas*

Fresh snow often drifts against a tent until it leans upon your hip like a fat and drunken friend. Shoving it off sleepily from within a warm down bag merely helps the next heavy snowfall collapse the whole damn thing. You lie awake for a minute, wondering if anyone from another tent has noticed. The silence says sadly not, but at least the wind has dropped. Having summoned the moral strength to deal with it yourself, you are soon dressed and breathless with lack of oxygen. Teeth chatter as you struggle with both hands to open a zip trapped within an icicle down its outside edge. 'This is going to be very, very unpleasant,' you murmur.

Stepping into the night air, you cannot believe your eyes. No clouds are left, not one. Just stars. Roughly a billion. And their light enough to see by. The mules stand about like sugared cakes, breathing the breath of dragons. Beyond them the crystal landscape rolls away from the mountain walls, disappearing gradually into deep dark blue. Utter silence is punctuated by the satisfying crunch of frozen snow underfoot as you make the rounds and, scraping each tent clear, muttered curses of rude awakenings are calmed by cosy gratitude. You don't hurry, but stand and stare in every direction, teeth gritted to stop yourself bellowing with the sheer joy of it. If you went for your camera you would wake your tent-mate yet again. The lens would steam up. In the twenty minutes needed to expose it correctly, the film might freeze and snap. To say nothing of your knees. The moment stays just that: a moment. One only you will see.

On jungle trails where light was dim and a coloured snake too fast, or a high plains village, golden-lit below an indigo sky in a horizontal downpour, and the fleeting smile on a shy girl's lips – how many other moments have passed unrecorded over the years? Thousands for every photograph in this book. Hundreds more failed in their execution, in the rush, in selection and, most painfully, in the final edit. A picture-driven book grows in all directions at once and when the time comes to prune it, a tree is standing where you thought you had planted a bush. Shears are traded for a chainsaw.

The words grow at a slower pace, more like bonsai really. Fed with memories, academic books and a compost of deadlines.

Peru has twenty-eight out of the thirty-two defined climates in the world, and of the 104 classified 'zones of life', eighty-four are found within its borders. The southeast encapsulates this variety, from brittle ice to sweltering jungle. With nearly all the major Inca ruins including Machu Picchu, two of the world's finest white-water rafting rivers, Lake Titicaca, the most pristine rainforest in the Americas, the source of the Amazon *and* the highest biological diversity on the planet, it can safely be said that this area is unparalleled on earth. But it is beyond the beaten track of ruins and reserves that I find my favourite images. Up impassable roads you ditch the car and walk, sliding down mountain streams you find the unseen view, and behind the battered doors, barking dogs and courtyards, family heirlooms are unwrapped with twinkling eyes. Cuzco is my home from home, surrogate university, where godchildren grow and dear friends lie buried. Among these people and landscapes, festivals, textures and light, I found the impossibility of boredom. Magic details lived and trapped, the moments that make up this book.

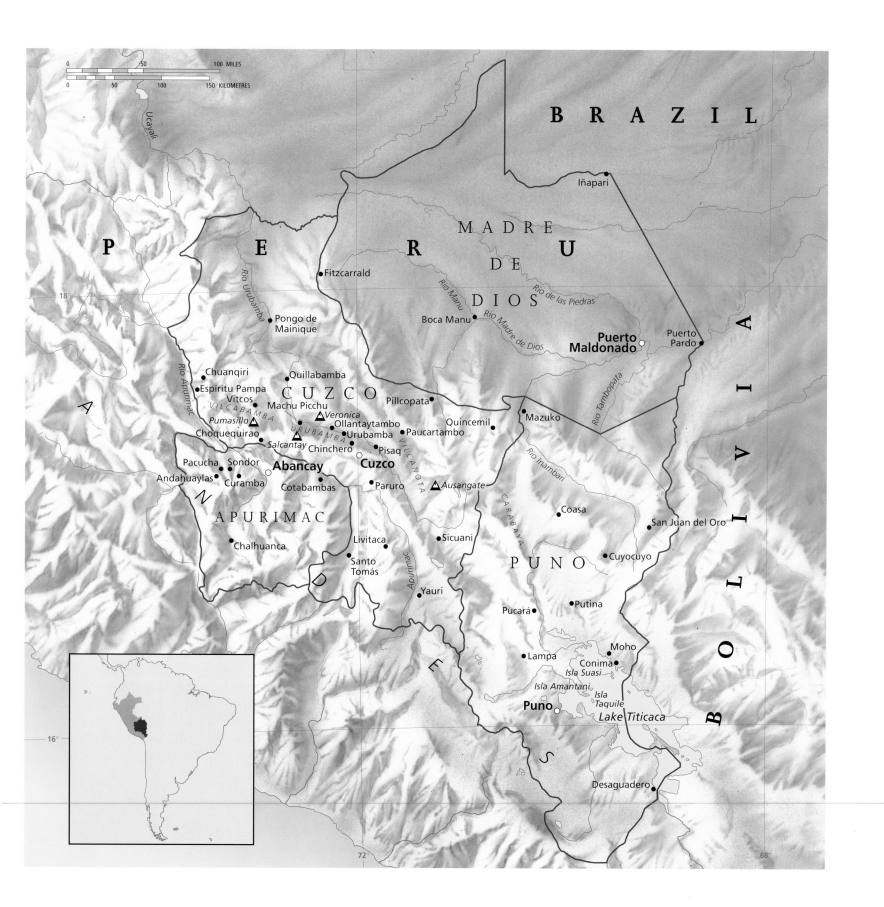

BRAZIL

PERU

Ucayali

MADRE

DE

DIOS

Iñapari

Río Urubamba

Fitzcarrald

Río Manu

Río de las Piedras

18°

Pongo de
Mainique

Boca Manu

Río Madre de Dios

Puerto
Maldonado

Puerto
Pardo

Río Apurímac

Chuanqiri

Quillabamba

CUZCO

Pillcopata

Espíritu Pampa
Vitcos
Machu Picchu
Pumasillo △ Veronica
Choquequirao
Salcantay
△
Chinchero
Pacucha Sondor
Andahuaylas
Curamba
Cotabambas

Ollantaytambo
Urubamba
Pisaq
Cuzco
Paruro

VILCABAMBA

URUBAMBA

Abancay

Quincemil

Paucartambo

Mazuko

Río Tambopata

VILCANOTA

△ Ausangate

Coasa

San Juan del Oro

Río Inambari

CARABAYA

Chalhuanca

APURIMAC

Livitaca

Santo
Tomás

Apurímac

Sicuani

Yauri

PUNO

Cuyocuyo

Putina

Pucará

Lampa

Moho
Conima
Isla Suasi

Isla Amantani

Puno

Isla
Taquile

Lake Titicaca

BOLIVIA

Desaguadero

16°

72°

68°

1 ABOVE THE CLOUDS

Gods and Glaciers

I can't exaggerate the beauty of the empty whiteness, stretching from height to height, or the brilliance of the snow in the sun, or the elliptical, magnesium-blue loops of shadow.

PATRICK LEIGH FERMOR *Three Letters from the Andes*

To the native Indian of Peru, the continual sight of the snow-howdahed Andes conveys naught of dread, except, perhaps, in the mere fancy of the eternal frosted desolateness reigning at such vast altitudes, and the natural conceit of what a fearfulness it would be to lose oneself in such inhuman solitudes.

HERMAN MELVILLE *Moby Dick*

In southern Peru any visit to the snowline has something of the pilgrimage or expedition about it. Standing only eleven degrees south of the equator, the permafrost begins at over 14,700 feet (4,500m); a height not arrived at by chance. In the thin air, the simple functions of legs and lungs become conscious acts, the placing of one foot in front of the other a technique requiring some concentration. After any significant time on the peaks themselves, at over 20,300 feet (6,200m), frostbite, hypothermia or edema will eventually take their toll. At these altitudes, the human body from tip to toe simply begins to die.

Still rising imperceptibly, with the occasional shudder, the Andes divide the driest place on earth from one of the wettest. The Atacama desert, on the coastal plain, has areas where rain has never been recorded, and yet the cloud forest on the eastern slopes receives an average 20 feet (6m) annual rainfall (six times greater than soggy Britain). These mountains are life-giving, but global warming is diminishing their power. The river Amazon begins here in pools of molten ice, but the accelerating rate at which the glaciers retreat is alarming. As each of these rivers and streams feeds Amazonia with mineral-enriched water, the ramifications of their continued decline are as grave as the deforestation below.

The Snow Peaks were the most powerful earthly deities in Inca times and the four ranges of Vilcanota, Vilcabamba, Carabaya and Urubamba are venerated to this day. Prayers to Christ and the Virgin often include the name of the nearest Apu (mountain god), and offerings are made to them from the highest altiplano to the depths of the forests. Ausangate (20,939 feet/6,384m) and Salcantay (20,568 feet/ 6,271m) are the highest mountains and most sacred Apus in the south.

At the high passes between mountains, cairns called *apacitas* stand 6 feet (1.8m) high, made of small rocks carried from distances below as acts of faith or contrition, or for luck. Often desolate places with fierce funnelled wind, the pillars imbue them with a comforting gauge of the humanity that has passed that way; thousands of journeys and moments of contemplation made tangible in stone. When clouds swirl up from the lowlands and envelop them, they can even look like people; indeed, the farmers below build similar structures on their enclosure walls to scare puma and foxes – straps of noisily flapping plastic make them even more convincing – and the *arrieros* (mule wranglers) will recount the embarrassing tale for years if you are caught calling out to one in the mist.

Stepping into the first snow is always exhilarating, whether clambering out of a vehicle at a mountain pass chapel-shrine or, more so, arriving step by step on an arduous and remote Inca trail. The glistening untouched surface and chilled lack of oxygen add to the light-headed impression of magical other-worldliness. There is no sign of humanity, the landscape a blank canvas, and a childlike exuberance explodes with the impact of snowballs and the tingling shock of snow on skin. These antics aren't restricted solely to boorish trekkers; the *arrieros* pride themselves on accuracy (they are also deadly with a sling and stone) and take great delight in getting someone else blamed for a good headshot.

The *arrieros* are invariably young men from communities along the lower stretches of the trail, led by elder villagers who may own the mules. These are tough individuals, taut-muscled, with leather hands and sun-parched faces that break into wide conspiratorial grins about recent mishaps, a glorious view, the latest bawdy joke or the time they caught the gringo talking to a tall pile of rocks. Their knowledge of terrain, trails and what the weather might do are inspirational, and their contagious humour will switch from Spanish to Quechua, when the odd, choice phrases referring to acts of human multiplication precede great guffaws from the elder ones and hand-covered grins from the youngest. There is a gentleness to them that springs partly from a great love and reverence for the landscape, and partly from the profound melancholy that permeates the conquered Andean nations. Their sadness is revealed in their *huayno* songs, the lyrics always referring to loss and heartbreak, and an idyllic time now past.

With snow falling they hurriedly construct a shelter for themselves out of saddles, sheepskins and hides, a plastic sheet roof pulled over and tucked underneath. Tourists sometimes worry that they don't use tents – their concern is needless. With the blue flame of a stove or glowing charcoal embers, their makeshift home soon has a feeling of permanence. Ponchos, blankets, hides and girths keep them from the freezing ground, and bottles and knick-knacks litter the floor; even the smell

of sweat and horses seems comforting. Up to ten of them may be in there, gently mocking the youngest recruits or listening to a *huayno* or football match on a tiny transistor radio. They have no use for synthetic two-man tents.

Their usual cargo may be coffee beans or potatoes, but they enjoy the relaxed enthusiasm of trekking groups and certainly the tips are better. The behaviour of inexperienced gringos is also a constant source of amusement. On exploratory hikes over 16,400 feet (5,000m), the lack of oxygen felt in the day can be heightened at night by the shallow breath of sleep. You awake, half suffocated, with a loud roaring gasp. In a dark, confined space, your blind thrashings can cause potent shock in a drowsing tent-mate, whose reactions may be even more boisterous. It can take quite some time for you both to pull yourselves together before it happens again half an hour later. Neither repetition nor exhaustion dulls the spontaneity, but the atmosphere is slightly improved if you take it in turns. The ensuing giggles from the *arrieros'* encampment only add to the festive atmosphere of escalating frustration.

Treading slowly upwards, with pounding lungs and freezing sweat, staring at your feet, counting out your steps, the question 'Why the hell am I doing this?' is never far from the lips. Hours later, as you stride into camp, the hardships are balanced out, and not merely by a sense of achievement. The experiences of isolation, and interaction with a medieval culture, are a rare delight. Views and encounters are etched on the mind for the rest of your life, and you get a good, long, panoramic look at yourself as well as at the vast lifeless landscapes. Like the great oceans and deserts of the world, mountains are intruded upon and one always leaves them in some way humbled.

The festival of Qollur Rit'i or Snow Star takes place at just over 15,000 feet (4,700m) in the Vilcanota range. Originally relating to the annual reappearance of the Pleiades constellation around June 9th, the festival was Christianized in 1780 when Mariano Mayta, a lonely shepherd boy, had a miraculous vision of a white Christ child with whom he played. When men came to grab the apparition, he turned into a crucifix, at which Mariano dropped dead with grief. The church built around the rock where Mariano died became the focus of the pilgrimage, whose date became tied to Corpus Christi; a portrait of Christ on the rock within the church is the venerated Señor de Qollur Rit'i. Tens of thousands of pilgrims walk for up to five days to reach the shrine, where they leave offerings and requests; they dance in a frenzy of sleep deprivation, fireworks and bitter cold for three days and nights. During the day, some of the pilgrims climb up to the glacier base to say prayers (below).

On the moonlit glaciers of Mount Qolquepunku (right), Ukukus (immortal bear-men, representing fertility) defy the Kukuchi (invisible cannibalistic souls condemned to roam the ice fields) by retrieving crosses left there at the start of the festivities. As first light strikes the glacier, the Ukukus kneel and murmur prayers to the rising sun, the Apus (mountain gods) and the Señor de Qollur Rit'i.

Their triumphant return with crosses and huge chunks of sacred ice (above and front cover) brings the ritual chaos of the pilgrimage to a harmonious end, guaranteeing fertility and rebirth for the coming year, which began for the Incas on the June 21st winter solstice.

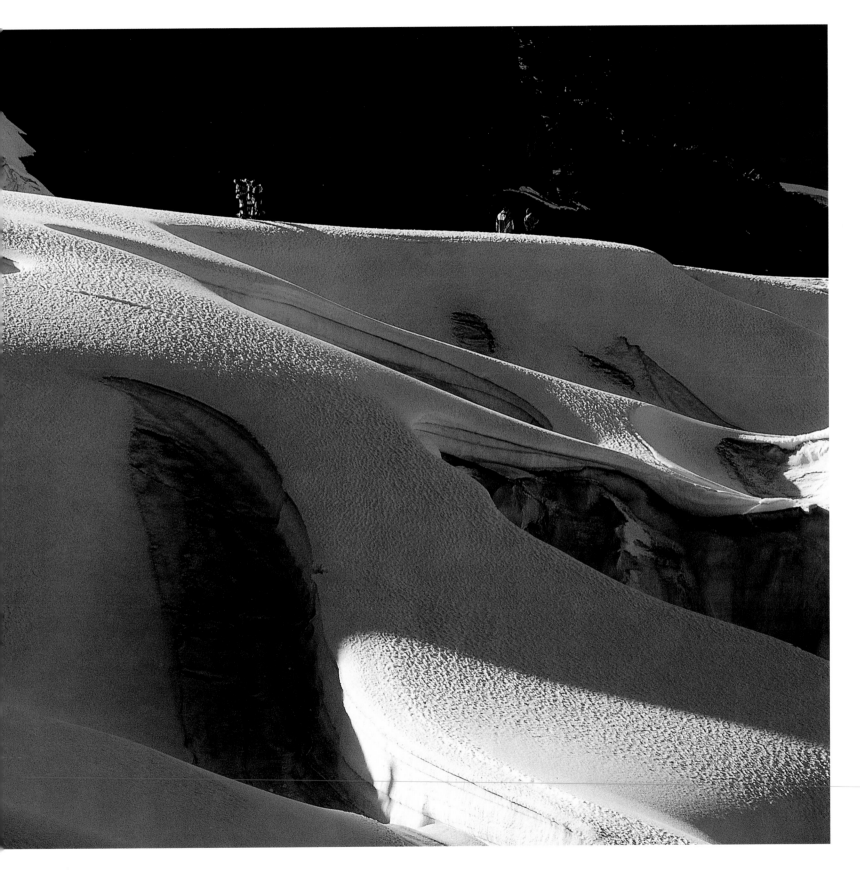

The last Ukukus descend in single file from the three glaciers surrounding the Sinakara valley (left). Only Ukukus are allowed on to the glacier itself and all of them are men. The tongue of ice and empty ravine at the bottom left of the main photograph show how much the glaciers are retreating each year due to climate change; the amount of ice removed during the festival, however, is negligible. A recent ban on the collection of ice lasted for only one season as the Ukukus took to carrying large rocks down the mountain in a substitute act of penance. The acts of faith carried out throughout the pilgrimage are all the more remarkable for the total lack of amenities available at the site, a factor that thankfully keeps mass tourism at bay, though some purists complain that the festival has already been changed by the influx of urban middle-class dance groups. Occasionally someone dies of cold or a fall, and this is considered a payment to Pacha Mama (Mother Earth) and a good omen for the year ahead. The practice of human sacrifice remains firmly in the imagination of the odd foreign journalist.

With bells jingling and llama foetus bouncing along behind, a dancer in the costume of Qapaq Colla leads his son from the base of the glacier to the church shrine below (above). The Collas were the llama-herding and wool-trading tribe that lived around the Titicaca region to the south and were conquered early in the Inca expansion. They are distinguished from the Ukukus by their flat rectangular beaded hats and white balaclava masks.

Chapel shrines (left) are often found where roads reach mountain passes. Drivers and passengers pay their respects to iconic embroidered crosses representing the communities from which they come. Their journeys between the jungle and mountain towns are made hazardous by the cliff-lined routes and the habit of driving at night; sadly, not all prayers are heard. Several thousand feet below this chapel at Abra Málaga, on the descent to Quillabamba from the Sacred Valley, stands an altogether more pagan shrine in a cloud forest river that vehicles must cross. A rock in midstream is festooned with flowers, thrown there to appease *sirenas* (mermaids) who it is said tempt drivers to eternal limbo.

On the last night of Qollur Rit'i, before the retrieval of the crosses, fireworks streak in every direction from tall bamboo towers (above). The sparks, flames and explosions that sometimes strike the heart of the candle-bearing crowd are considered to be part of the ritual chaos and are usually the cause of much hilarity. Injuries are rarely serious and add to the atmosphere of endurance.

Fresh snow covers the grazing grounds of llama and alpaca on the approach to the Arapa pass beneath the northwestern flank of Mount Ausangate (right). The dry-stone-walled enclosure is used during the annual round-up of animals for shearing. As well as being the most sacred Apu, the mountain provides one of the best trekking opportunities in southern Peru. On an eight-day trek supported by llamas or mules around the base of the mountain, groups pass varied landscapes (above), making stops at weaving villages and natural hot springs.

Barefooted but for the open rubber sandals known as *ojotas*, María Teresa, a shepherd girl, stands proudly astride a snowman (left). Intermittently she throws small rocks at a black bull to drive it off the potato patch; several sheep stand huddled in the lee of a wall, and her mother grins from within the darkness of their windowless house. They live a long day's walk from the nearest village and are as amazed and amused by a foreigner and his camera as I am to see someone building a snowman in a snowstorm in the high Andes.

Each of the major peaks dominates its area spiritually and physically. Offerings and prayers, even Christian ones, are often preceded with the name of the nearest Apu. This page: part of the Pumasillo mountain, swathed in cloud at sunset, from Minas Victoria (top left). Mount Chimboya with a fresh dusting of snow (top right). Salcantay on a clear evening from the Mollepata trail (bottom right). Ausangate from the Tinqui approach; a pair of *huallata*, Andean geese, call mournfully across the desolate *puna*, high plateau (bottom left).

This page: a small herd of alpaca in front of the classic northern profile of Ausangate (top left). Mount Veronica's peak appears briefly among hail-bearing clouds. Also known as Huacay Huilca, meaning the god who cries, due to the streams and avalanches that come off the mountain (top right). Pumasillo in the last light of day (bottom right). Ninamarca in the eastern Vilcanota range (bottom left).

Laguna Sibinacocha (left). At 16,400 feet (5,000m), the 14-mile (22.5km) long lagoon is an impressive sight, its northern end surrounded by four dramatic peaks. To the south stands the largest ice field in the region, just to the left of this reflected view. The lagoon has few fish, but enough organic material to sustain a large seasonal population of Chilean flamingos. The few human inhabitants of the area are alpaca grazers. Their houses (top right) are sunlit at the far left of the shoreline, the waters darkened by an approaching snowstorm. The endangered vicuña can also be seen here in small groups, usually as fleeing silhouettes against the horizon.

On Laguna Hatun Pucacocha, or Big Red Lagoon (so called because of the red shale slopes reflected in its usually still waters), a lump of fallen glacial ice briefly takes on the appearance of Pegasus (bottom right). The sound of a massive ice avalanche tumbling down into the lagoon at night is one of the hair-raising wonders of an Andean trek. Most lake names end with 'cocha' which is something of a tautology, as it means 'lake' in Quechua; but, as noted by those who study the local weavings, the word actually refers to the physical bowl holding the waters, not the water itself.

Arrieros or wranglers blindfold the pack mules with their colourful cummerbunds before loading them (top). It stops them wandering off as the different layers of hide, blanket and saddle are tied on, and placates them while the others are rounded up. The *arrieros* are extremely hardy; their ubiquitous *ojota* sandals are made from old car tyres and I have never seen one wear socks. The stacked saddles to the right are the dismantled walls of the shelter in which they spent the night.

Levitating tablecloths are one of the hazards of a high altitude breakfast (above). The length of time needed to boil a kettle is another.

Though the lead mules' forelegs are hobbled at night, a pre-dawn round-up is a regular event (right). The gentle cursing of the wranglers' '*¡Mula carajo!*' resounds between valley walls, as the first light of dawn mingles with full moonlight over a hail-strewn landscape and Mount Salcantay's southern flank.

A mule train descends from the Choquetacarpo pass at 15,000 feet (4,600m) towards the *puna*, dry canyons and cloud forests of Vilcabamba (left). This particular trek, to the ruins of Choquequirao, passes through five distinct habitats and climates. Mules and horses better serve treks ending at lower altitudes than llamas. They also carry more than twice the weight of a cameloid.

Set in the desolate granite landscape, the windowless thatched stone houses warmed by burnt dung are reminiscent of those of medieval Scottish highlanders. The pastoral care of wool-bearing animals and the diet of potatoes, along with the use of woven patterns in ponchos to denote one's origins, add to this impression.

At the La Raya pass, at 14,147 feet (4,313m) between Cuzco and Puno,
the Carabaya range stretches away to the south, on the eastern flank of
the divide. From here, the river Urubamba flows north and the watershed
of the Titicaca basin flows south.

Glacial moraine at the base of Mount Ausangate. Though the sculptural landscape of these multicoloured clays is a delight for the eye, the build-up of it on one's boots can be exhausting. On this week-long trek, the landscape changes dramatically each day.

An *arriero* encourages a llama train to cross an icy stream flowing from the glacier behind (above). Abuse hurled in Quechua and Spanish is often followed by a small rock. A direct hit on a leading llama's backside has the desired effect.

After a thaw, another of Ausangate's landscapes is revealed (right). The white dots grazing on the *puna* below are alpacas, bred for their extremely fine wool. Each of the rivers and streams here eventually feeds into the Amazon and the Atlantic Ocean some 3,000 miles (4,800km) away.

2 ALTIPLANO

The High Plains and Canyons

Maguey cactus, your heart is without honey, and it is sad,
with the same sadness that we feel, we men of Peru …
you stand straight and true, close to our anguish, along
the infinite roads that stretch ahead.

CIRO ALEGRÍA *Broad and Alien is the World*

The sound of the Apurimac rises faintly from the gorge,
like a murmur from outer space … 'Apurimac river!
Apurimac river!' the Runa children repeat with tenderness
and a touch of fear.

JOSÉ MARÍA ARGUEDAS *Los Ríos Profundos*

The appearance of the highlands in the golden age of the Incas can barely be imagined in today's rustic chaos. When the Inca – God-King – reigned supreme, there was order in everything. Spectacular feats of engineering and irrigation triumphed over one of the most barren environments on earth, supporting the cultivation of an area four times greater than the area farmed today.

The initial spread of Tahuantinsuyo (as the empire was known) from Cuzco was gradual and peaceful up until the massive expansion after 1430. Even then some cultures joined without bloodshed, albeit under the threat of a vast disciplined army. The eastern rainforest proved impenetrable but no real problem, and trade was established with tribes such as the Machiguenga who also provided great archers. In the north and south, however, the fighting never ended. The real strength of the Inca state lay in efficient administration; it made an art form of harnessing manpower within a strong hierarchical social system. Large-scale relocation made hostages and garrisons of newly conquered tribes, whose leaders' sons were taken to Cuzco and married into Inca nobility. Taxes in the form of state labour and tributes kept the network of paved roads and agricultural terraces perfectly maintained, while the storehouses were filled with sufficient cloth, weapons and food to sustain the entire population through times of war or famine. Movement throughout the empire was strictly controlled and regional costumes were encouraged in order to develop identity.

Great festivals known as *Raymis* punctuated the Inca calendar, uniting the disparate highland cultures. At times of sowing and harvest, as well as at the solstices and equinoxes, elaborate ceremony and ritual enforced the status of the deified Inca. Authority founded in small village councils called *ayllus* climbed the pyramid of power up to the Sapa Inca, Son of the Sun. It was a curious mix of despotism and patriarchal care. No one wanted for shelter, work or basic meals, including the elderly, blind and crippled who were found duties they could perform. Private property was an unknown concept, for which there were and are no Quechua words. Every citizen was a part of the ordered whole, their lives interlocked by duty like the fluid masonry of their walls. '*Ama suwa, ama qella, ama lulla*' – 'Don't lie, don't steal, don't be lazy'– was a common greeting; 'Nor you', the reply.

It is almost inconceivable, then, that an army of 169 men could conquer the largest empire in the Americas, but the timing of the Spanish incursion coincided with a series of catastrophes that left Tahuantinsuyo vulnerable. A mysterious epidemic, possibly European smallpox introduced during the invasion of Mexico, had killed tens of thousands, including the Inca Huayna Qapaq, his heir Ninan Cuyuchi and much of the Inca court. The ensuing civil war waged between his sons Huascar and Atahualpa lasted several years. Then, at the moment of Atahualpa's triumph, the strange bearded white men arrived.

The speed of Tahuantinsuyo's expansion was its weakness. Many of the northern civilizations still saw the Incas as hostile invaders, so the Spanish were able to raise auxiliaries from battle-hardened tribes such as the Canari and Chachapoyans. In the sixteenth century, Spanish soldiers were some of the finest in the world, their weapons and strategies honed on campaigns against the Moors and Aztecs. The Incan armies, though disciplined and well led, relied on the devices of a bygone era: slingshot and bronze against arquebus and steel. The blast of cannon and arquebus would have horrified people whose gods included Thunder, but the greatest shock was the appearance and speed of the horse, an animal previously unknown in Peru. Though born of desperation, the Europeans' repeated tactic of full-scale unprovoked attack against seemingly impossible odds was extremely effective. In doing this from the outset, they immediately captured the Inca, neutralizing his recently victorious armies during the eight months it took to gather his ransom.

The empire of Tahuantinsuyo, for all its material trappings, was fundamentally metaphysical in outlook. A vision of the cosmos placed Cuzco at the centre of the world, with the Vilcanota/Urubamba river connecting with the Milky Way beyond the horizon. The landscape in its entirety was sacred, from the Apus in the highest peaks and deepest gorges to the *Tirakuna*, 'those who watch over us', embodied in every boulder, cave, lake and stream. Omens of the foreign invasion were all bad. A comet seen by Atahualpa (recorded in contemporary China) was taken as a portent of his impending death. Though Pizarro protested this was not true, Atahualpa was garrotted only thirteen days later (his father's demise had also followed the appearance of a comet). The sensation of predestined doom was accentuated by

the ancient belief that white men appearing from the sea would come as saviours. (Elderly Runa still greet whites with the term *Viracocha*, meaning Creator-God.)

A passage in the Huarochiri manuscript found in 1608 describes the observation in Inca times of the rising Pleiades in relation to crop cultivation. The constellation was called *Qollqa*, meaning storehouse. When Gary Urton was researching his book *At the Crossroads of the Earth and the Sky* in 1979, he spoke with a young boy about that year's disastrously late planting of potatoes, the staple diet. The boy was closely watching the rising Pleiades. When Urton asked him why, the answer was simple, 'Because we want to live'.

That story illustrates the continuing strength of traditional beliefs in Runa lives, but more tellingly that their lives have not improved since the utterly destructive actions of the conquest. A failed harvest without the patriarchal protection of the Inca state became a life-threatening affair, and remains so to this day. The intense shock felt when ordered sanctity was replaced by brutal greed left a profound melancholy that still permeates many aspects of Andean life.

Change is ageless – the pre-Inca ruins of the Canas, Chancas and Huari attest to that – but the pace of it grows faster. The cowboy culture of the Chumbivilcas plains has been replaced by bicycles and trucks; and the status symbol of concrete replaces adobe, even in the graveyards. Other changes are more disturbing: evangelists claim that llamas are 'unclean' because they are not mentioned in the Bible, thus encouraging the more destructive grazing of sheep. And when television documentary crews pay cash to alter festivals for better footage, they seem unaware that their changes remain, perhaps for other payments and other films.

The self-sufficiency encouraged by the Inca state still lingers on. Beyond the reach of road and pylon, vestiges of medieval culture endure. Reciprocal labour and worship of the landscape still define lifestyles. These altiplano realms are isolated from media-led democracy, separated from the society of modern Peru. In 1609, Garcilaso de la Vega, son of a Spanish captain and an Inca lady, referred to Peru as 'Stepmother to her children'. These last Peruvian Runa are orphans now, the living remnants of vibrant tribal cultures once united by a great civilization, then estranged in perpetuity by the sword and the cross, and the foreign capital on the coast.

The vast terraced sinkholes at Moray, on the Maras plain, were used as agricultural laboratories by the Incas who experimented with different strains of plants, particularly maize. Within these natural formations (the largest of the four is over 100 feet/30m deep), the temperature range between top and bottom can be as great as 27˚F (15˚C). Using terraces to accentuate shaded areas and capture maximum heat in others, the Incas were able to replicate many of the climate zones of the empire. This enabled them to cultivate an extraordinary variety of plants, some of which would usually perish at this altitude of nearly 11,150 feet (3,400m). (In 1987, a tiny sinkhole only 10 feet (3m) wide, but far above the tree line at 12,500 feet (3,800m), was found to contain subtropical plants; the dynamics of shelter from wind and capture of heat deserve further study.)

In the distance, between the dry plain and the darker foothills, lies the Sacred Valley of the Incas. The snow peak, San Juan, and adjoining glacier, Chicon, loom above the town of Urubamba, which gives its name to both the river and the range of mountains. Far left is the peak of Media Luna.

A typically deep ravine in the Cordillera Vilcabamba (top left). The two horses at the far left provide some sense of scale. The descent and climb to this spot was a four-hour walk from the snow at the base of Mount Salcantay seen in the distance.

Tres Cañones in the remote province of Espinar (bottom left). There are actually four canyons, one of which brings the headwaters of the Apurimac from Cailloma, the source of the Amazon.

The Chinchero plain lies between Cuzco and the Sacred Valley. The pyramid-shaped peak of Veronica (aka Huacay Huilca – God Who Cries) dominates the valley between Ollantaytambo and Machu Picchu (top left). To the right is the peak of Helancoma.

On the heavily cultivated Maras plain, a farmer herds sheep and three donkeys loaded with the dried stalks left after the maize harvest (bottom left). The donkeys have spent the day walking round and round separating wheat from chaff with their hooves. The farmer then winnows the remains with the long rake on his shoulder.

Huaypo lake surrounded by the intensely farmed land of the Chinchero plain (top right). Fields are still ploughed with oxen, and crops planted with the *chaquitaclla*, a local foot-plough. A broken-down combine harvester stands like an abstract sculpture in the corner of the main square of nearby Maras; it has been there for ten years.

Pre-Inca *chullpas* (burial towers) at Nimarca near Paucartambo are aligned between two large snow peaks, showing that mountain worship took place 1,000 years before the emergence of the Inca state (bottom right). Each one stands about 9 feet (2.7m) high and would have contained a family group. Looters have left nothing within them.

The province of Chumbivilcas is famous for the harshness of its terrain and the formidable nature of its inhabitants, particularly the highland cowboys. The massive dry-stone walls are almost a symbol of their attempt to tame the land (left). The biggest change to the landscape since the conquest occurred in 1968 when a left-wing military government led by General Velasco forced through the agrarian reform, whereby all the estates were confiscated from the landed families and distributed among the peasants. It was an unmitigated disaster, with poor management leading to a massive downturn in productivity. When asked about possible condor sightings here, a man answers, 'Before the reform there were nearly forty pairs; since the thousands of animals farmed here have dwindled, the condors have moved on. Velasco!' He spits, and gestures to the ruined hacienda with goats living upstairs and pigs below.

A horseman gallops past a *bosque de piedra* (rock forest) near Yauri (above). There are many strange and wonderful rock formations throughout the region, from stalactite-filled caves at Livitaca, to the cone-shaped sandstone spires of Pampachiri in Apurimac.

Corrals at the San Antonio dairy in Chumbivilcas (below). Before the agrarian reform they would have been filled with livestock. The landowner, who retains a tiny percentage of his family's old estate, escaped execution by one of the notorious Sendero Luminoso kangaroo courts due to the testimony of workers and neighbours who spoke of his gentlemanly conduct and skill as a vet. Sendero Luminoso, the Maoist terrorist organization, disbanded after the capture of its leader in the early 1990s.

Don Baltasar (below), a *jinete* or horseman, in full dress; these outfits are nowadays worn only at festivals and markets. Working horses too are a rare sight, having been replaced by bicycles and mopeds.

Don Baltasar canters across Machu Puente, or Old Bridge (right). This colonial Spanish structure spans the narrow canyon headwaters of the Apurimac, the source of the Amazon. Being the only crossing for miles, the small village that has grown there is known by the same name.

The tack room of the San Antonio dairy in Chillioroya (above). Hand-made cheeses are taken once a week to the shops and markets of Cuzco, eight hours' drive away. Here, at least, the cows are still rounded up on horseback.

The hacienda at Machu Puente (below) was built in the traditional colonial style of Espinar, with neat pebble paving, stonework and thatched whitewashed buildings. Its origins, however, are early twentieth century, an architectural tribute to an era long gone.

In the Chillioroya valley in Chumbivilcas, a hidden cave reveals this dramatic spouting stream (left). Like any unusual physical feature, it is considered sacred by local people. The cliffs surrounding it are full of nesting Andean geese and viscachas, a type of chinchilla, which lollop about and bounce up the sheer walls like furry cannonballs.

Q'eshwachaka, meaning 'grass-rope bridge', spanning the Apurimac canyon, is the last example of an Inca-style hanging bridge (above). Like the infamous 'Bridge of San Luis Rey', whose collapse further downstream was immortalized by Thornton Wilder, it is made of thickly woven ichu grass. The chosen artisans who weave and build the structure are known as the *chaka camayocs* – keepers of the bridge. The term *camayoc* is generally used in Quechua to describe an innate skill that one is born with, similar to the Spanish term *maestro*. Until recently, the annual replacement of the bridge took place at Epiphany in January. A North American documentary film crew once paid the villagers to do it in June, in the dry season, and this date has now become an annual 'traditional festival' for tourists to visit.

Apurimac (God Who Speaks) is the name given to the river, the canyon and the provincial department that borders them. Carving its way through granite, its rapids provide some of the best white-water rafting in the world (right). Though there is some debate about rival claims based on quantities of water dispersed, the Apurimac's claim as being the true source of the Amazon is based on distance from the Atlantic mouth.

Winnowing tarwi, a relative of the bean, and a high-altitude staple (above). Other high Andean plants like quinoa and kiwicha have been found to be extremely nutritious, containing extraordinary amounts of protein. NASA has used them in space food and they are becoming popular in health-food snackbars.

The potato originally came from Peru, where there are over 200 species and some 5,000 varieties. Here, an old man from Ocongate sorts a very sweet tuber called oca (below). Frozen by the ground temperature, the children eat them like ice-lollies.

A family in the Patacancha valley harvest potatoes (right). Chuño is a type of potato that is freeze-dried in the baking sun and frozen nights, to be used at any time. The sacks are woven from unrefined llama wool, each stripe the colour of the animal from which it came.

Llamas (*Lama glama*) and alpacas (*Lama pacos*) can be distinguished from each other by the llamas' longer ears and noses, and the alpacas' woollier heads and legs. Both species were domesticated several thousand years ago by pre-Inca herding societies, especially in the highlands of Puno, and are descended from wild guanacos (*Lama guanicoe*), which are now rare in Peru, though plentiful in Patagonia. The fourth cameloid is the vicuña (*Vicugna vicugna*) whose wool is the finest. The vicuña came close to extinction before recent efforts were made to save it, especially at the Pampas Galleras reserve, now named after Barbara D'Achille, an environmental journalist slain by Maoist terrorists in 1989.

The Incas had no need to invent the wheel, chiefly because cameloids will not pull any form of carriage (bulls and horses, as well as sheep, arrived with the Spanish). As pack animals, llamas were used to support and sustain the ever-expanding empire. They were also used for meat, wool and religious sacrifices. Alpaca wool was notably finer and, as weavings were one of the most valued commodities, had a superior status and value that continues to this day. It is worth mentioning here that weavings, foodstuffs and llamas were by far the most common sacrificial materials. Human sacrifice, though by no means unknown, was far rarer than in the Mayan and Aztec cultures to the north.

Llamas with ceremonial ear-tassels in their typical *puna* domain over 13,000 feet/4,000m (far left, top). They are haughty and display considerable arrogance towards anything that isn't another llama. Note the herders' windowless thatched house made of mud and stone in the background, a style unchanged in centuries.

Vicuñas (top left) are the smallest and most elegant of the species. A cousin of the guanaco, their pale brown wool is one of the finest in the world. Vicuña wool and hide products were prohibited for many years, but under careful management are re-entering the world's markets, as the population steadily increases.

Alpacas at a ranch and research centre in the department of Puno (bottom left). The commercial value of alpaca knitwear places them at the centre of an international multi-million-dollar industry. Along with llamas they are becoming popular pets, especially in the United States.

Guanacos, the largest New World cameloid (far left, bottom), still live in the wild and are the closest relative to the common ancestor of African and Arabic camels, a North American beast now extinct.

Maucallacta, meaning 'Place of the Ancestors' in Quechua (there are several sites so named), stands on the banks of the headwaters of the Apurimac river (far left). It is protected on two sides by dramatic pink-pillared cliff formations. Rarely visited due to its remoteness in the province of Espinar, very little is known about its creators.

A false-domed *chullpa* at Maucallacta (left). Though the arch was unknown until the conquest, there are several examples of false domes and corbelled roofs in pre-Inca architecture.

Standing at a slight incline on a high plateau, the winds at K'anamarca (right and overleaf) can be ferocious. The round structures are thought to have been used for storage. Subsequently, after Inca expansion, round structures were usually associated with buildings of great religious importance, like the Sun temples of Cuzco, Machu Picchu and Pisaq.

K'anamarca was built by the Canas tribe, who still inhabit the high plains surrounding Yauri. The apparent Inca influence in some of the buildings is hotly denied by proud descendants of the Canas who claim that, on the contrary, the Canas influenced Inca architecture. Some of the structures are still in use by llama and potato-growing farmers, which give this stunning ruin an atmosphere unlike any other.

The highlands were the cradle of many highly developed pre-Inca civilizations (as was the coastal plain). These pages show examples of architecture from the Middle Horizon period of South American archaeology (AD 600–1000), through to a colonial Spanish town abandoned in the early twentieth century.

The defensively terraced hill temple of Sondor (top left), near Andahuaylas, is thought to have been a major sacred centre of the Chanca empire. It has breathtaking views on all sides, including the sacred Pacucha lake seen on page 3. A fierce battle raged here, won by the Incas whose classic trapezoidal niches are seen in their later buildings to the right and front. It was the defeat of the Chancas that initiated the massive expansion of the Inca empire.

At Curamba (far left, bottom), also in the Apurimac province of Andahuaylas, stands this little-known *usnu*, a terraced pyramid structure used to oversee gatherings by the Inca, who sat on a throne at the top. From here the Chanca temple of Sondor is visible on the horizon. Larger well-known examples of *usnus* stand at the administrative centres of Vilcashuaman in Ayacucho and Huánuco Pampa in the central highlands.

Apachaco (bottom left), near Yauri, is a colonial ghost town that is peculiar in its perfect balance of eeriness and charm. It was abandoned in the early 1900s after being struck by a plague-like disease. Flowers are still left at the base of the cross outside the church and in the tree-lined graveyard to the left. The pretty, naïve murals adorning the church's façade and the sounds of the river washing musically around the base of the surrounding pink cliffs only add to its haunting enchantment.

Piquillacta (Place of the Flea), was a large city of the Huari culture (right). It was the most important of five sites, each placed in an entrance to the Lucre basin, around Huarcapay lagoon, just south of Cuzco. Mystery surrounds its uses, especially as many of the rooms connect neither to corridors nor to each other. Since 1982, the archaeologist Gordon McEwen has studied this grid-planned ruin which covers three-quarters of a square mile (2 sq km) and is thought to have been built between AD 500 and 600. The vacuum left after the fall of the Huaris may have led to the initially peaceful spread of Inca culture, before the massive expansion after the Chanca war. This site is also noted for two sets of 40 turquoise figurines found buried here.

The *Chiaraje* is a ritual battle, named after the small plain where it is fought. Two communities of loosely connected villages send approximately 500 men to fight each other with fist-sized rocks fired from slings, and maces for close combat. The battles take place in early and late January and, as can be seen from the head-wounds, are fought in earnest. The two armies face each other from opposing hills surrounding the bowl-shaped valley. At first, horsemen ride out and taunt the opposition, then both armies attack and retreat repeatedly. Outflanking manoeuvres mean that there is nowhere safe for outsiders to watch; indeed, anthropologists have been attacked before the battle itself gets started. After a formal break for lunch when large quantities of alcohol are drunk, the mêlée of violence rages more harshly, with bystanders and even an ambulance crew coming under fierce attack. (A French television cameraman was seriously injured in 1999.) A death is seen as a payment of blood for Pacha Mama (Mother Earth), and the victim is given a festive hero's burial back in his home village. Similar bloodletting rituals take place in Bolivia and Ecuador where they are called *Tinku*, Quechua for an encounter.

Under the cover of clouds and fog, tactical charges and retreats are made, and stones collected into pouches (above). The accurate and rapid aim of the sling was used to great effect by the Incas in the sieges of Ollantaytambo and Cuzco, including the killing of Juan Pizarro at the battle of Sacsayhuaman.

A horseman with an industrial-bolt-headed mace pulls up his horse after a threatening false charge (top right). The speed of a horse is an advantage, but they are also obvious targets. A man winded by a fall is extremely vulnerable to a mace attack by infantry.

A piper playing a *chark'a*, a locally named *pinkillu* flute made from the *kantuta* tree (bottom right). Usually they are bound with llama gut, not black rubber. With a bloodied jacket from an ear wound, he stands near the frontline. The air is filled with whistles, shouts and battle cries with the intermittent rain of rocks falling to the ground. The sound of stones whizzing past your head stays with you for days.

The most severe non-fatal injuries are broken femurs and smashed cheekbones. Headshots are a clear attempt at a kill, though this man (below) escaped merely grazed. Scars from previous years are borne with great pride.

During the festival of Cruz Velacuy at the beginning of May, crosses brought down from the hilltops where they stand all year are dressed with robes and flowers (left). They are a link between the Inca and Christian religions; a potent symbol of Christ, placed on mountains venerated long before the arrival of Europeans. In this tiny chapel belonging to a ruined hacienda, a tattered plastic flag symbolizes the modern nation of Peru.

Over the past 20 years, high-rise cement tombs have become a great status symbol for the departed (above). With the combined forces of Andean weather and rustic aesthetics, they soon blend into their surroundings. Andean graveyards invariably stand apart from the churches. With high walls and locked gates, they have a town-like quality of their own. On the Day of the Dead, November 2nd, they come alive to music, dance, tears and flowers (both real and plastic) that leave a jaunty ambience for months.

A typical highland figure in a town called Descanso, meaning 'rest' (right). The hand-woven trousers are fast disappearing, though the *ojota* sandals, nowadays made of car tyres, are a triumph of utilitarian fashion.

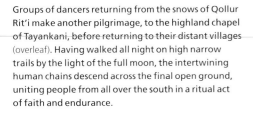

Groups of dancers returning from the snows of Qollur Rit'i make another pilgrimage, to the highland chapel of Tayankani, before returning to their distant villages (overleaf). Having walked all night on high narrow trails by the light of the full moon, the intertwining human chains descend across the final open ground, uniting people from all over the south in a ritual act of faith and endurance.

3   TITICACA

The Source

The Incas regarded the area with veneration. Their legends of the creation and
the flood took place on the mysterious lake.
JOHN HEMMING *The Conquest of the Incas*

All round the horizon, reminding us of the enormous altitude, the tops of cumulus
clouds come cauliflowering up from below. There is a mad feeling of dimensionless
vacancy in the air.
PATRICK LEIGH FERMOR *Three Letters from the Andes*

The term 'New World' for the Americas is apt, not just
because of its late discovery by Europeans, but because
of the late arrival of humanity itself. In Europe, Africa
and Asia, hunter-gatherers roamed as Homo Sapiens
from approximately 100,000 years ago. The oldest
surviving structure, a grave in Iraq, has been dated at
60,000 BC. Culture and Art as concepts began around
34,000 BC. Yet human beings arrived in South America
as late as 18,000 BC, having crossed the Bering Strait
only during the last ice age.

Lake Titicaca appears in the origin myths of most of
the region's Aymara- and Quechua-speaking cultures.
The Creator-God Viracocha appeared from the waters
and made the Sun, he ended darkness and began time.
It was also in this area of the southern highlands that
the llama, alpaca and highly nutritious guinea pig were
domesticated as well as beans, quinoa and potatoes.
These innovations laid the foundations from which all
subsequent advanced cultures were formed, from Pucará
to the Incas. Both history and legend concur that Titicaca
was the cradle of Andean civilization.

Apart from widespread references to a cataclysmic
flood, an event whose biblical resonances must have

pleased the Christian clerics who later recorded it,
the other great myth was that of Manco Qapaq, Son of
the Sun, and Mama Oqllo, Daughter of the Moon, who
were said to have risen from the waters of the lake and
appeared on Titi Caca Island (Titicaca means 'Rock of the
Cat' in Aymara), now called the Island of the Sun. From
here they marched north and founded Cuzco; he as first
Inca and she as his Coya, or royal Inca wife. The flood
scenario was thought for many years to have been a
reference to the last ice age. Recent discoveries appear to
suggest roots in more recent events.

Scientists from a number of US academic
institutions, including Duke, Stanford and the Woods
Hole Institute, have found evidence of massive and
repeated overflowing from the southern end of the
lake, occurring in cycles of 1–2,000 years. Examining
sediment at various depths, they found detailed
information going back 25,000 years. The driest period,
between 4000 and 3000 BC, dropped the surface to 250
feet (75m) lower than present levels, and yet since then
it has spilled over at various times, reaching the salt flats
of northern Bolivia and Chile. These floods would have
had an enormously destructive effect on civilizations

like Tiahuanaco on the southern shores of the lake; such events would have entered the lore of strong oral cultures. In AD 2000, an Italian-led expedition found extensive ruins under water near the islands of the Sun and Moon. Provisionally dated at between AD 500 and 1000, there are several huge structures, including one measuring 660 by 160 feet (200 x 50m) and a containing wall 2,600 feet (800m) long. It was certainly a site of great importance.

For reasons unknown, the collapse of the Tiahuanaco culture occurred around that time. This, and the fall of the Huari culture, left a power vacuum into which the Incas gradually expanded. Was the legendary march north to Cuzco of Manco Qapaq and Mama Oqllo based on the evacuation of these lands? The current theory is that the Incas invented the story solely to combine their religious origins with those of the more ancient Viracocha. But there is speculation that culturally advanced people moved north before the founding of Cuzco and that Aymara, not Quechua, might have been the lingua franca of the early elite. Certainly the word 'coca', applied to the sacred bush used in religious ceremonies to this day, comes from the Aymara term *khoka* meaning 'the tree'. At the moment all is supposition. Archaeological finds showing stronger links, for example ceramics, are lacking. Perhaps the lake still holds secrets.

Wilder suppositions place the famous Sun Disc of the Incas in an Eternal Etheric city on the bed of Lake Titicaca, built by legendary Lemurians, which will rise again before judgement day. Colonial accounts and chronicles last mention the 'Punchao', as the disc was known, being forfeited in a game of cards by thieving conquistadors. Many historians believe it lies in a vault under the Vatican, along with many other articles of Inca gold.

What is certain is that the Incas invaded the area with all their might some time after 1430. The local Colla tribe became great enemies of the Incas, rebelling fifty years before the Spanish arrived, and joining forces with the conquistadors with gusto. They were commercial herders and traders as opposed to the pastoral agriculturists of the Quechua-speaking tribes, and they are commemorated as a defeated foe in many festivals, as seen in Chapter 6. The pre-Inca cultures of Pucará, Tiahuanaco and Lupaca around the lake are most noted for their extraordinarily fine masonry techniques, and these were their most obvious contribution, as the Incas typically incorporated them into their own building style. When interrogated by Spaniards after the conquest about their role in Tahuantinsuyo, the Incan empire, local people replied, 'We used to go to Cuzco, to build houses for the Inca.'

The islands of Titicaca have an ethereal quality that captures all the aspects that make the lake famous: a rarefied atmosphere of bright brilliant light, infused with history and fable, and a stark simplicity. The small private island of Suasi on the northern side is the most remote; a nature reserve with a rustic lodge that is as close to paradise as I have been. Taquile and Amantani are easier to get to and provide a rare look at lives unchanged in millennia. The three- or four-hour boat trips remove these places from the outside world; the islands and mainland are transformed into thin lines on the horizon during the journey, adding a surreal element to the isolation. Each time I leave, there is a vaguely dreamlike quality to the whole experience. Admittedly, on the rare occasions of a squall the journey is less poetic, but the boatmen know better than to challenge the gods of the lake.

The island of Taquile offers an almost perfect continuation of an Inca lifestyle. A uniformly cooperative society, without crime, vehicles, horses or cows, creates an atmosphere all its own. At the school, the children recite the Inca greeting written above the blackboard: '*Ama suwa, ama qella, ama lulla*' (Don't lie, don't steal, don't be lazy). The absence of dogs (whose constant barking is usually the soundtrack of the Andean night) creates a silence that wraps around you like a quilt. Lying beneath a billion stars on a hilltop places you nearer them, with no horizon to give any sense of scale. Concentrate on one bright star and imagine it is Earth; soon with the norms of gravity and perspective removed, you become conscious of our spinning journey through space, the warm ground beneath your back, a strangely altered base, and all your life, friends, memories and possessions a million miles away upon a dot. Like looking off the edge of a cliff, the sensation afterwards is one of great reassurance. Should your behaviour be witnessed by passing islanders, have no fear; they will merely take you for harmless drunks or lovers.

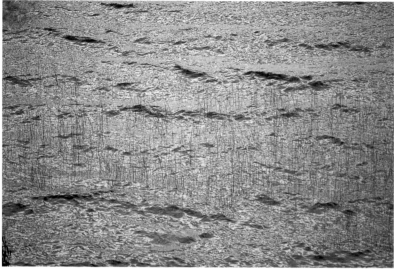

The views over Lake Umayo below Sillustani are as captivating as the pre-Inca burial *chullpas* that people have gone there to see (top left).

At Moho, quinoa is grown on the steep surrounding promontories, and the bays are lined with the floating cages of farmed trout (bottom left).

On the nature reserve island of Suasi, there is little to do but contemplate the changing play of wind and light on the water and vegetation: tall dry grasses, giant eucalyptus and the tortora reeds by the dry-stone dock (top right).

When the wind drops, the reeds appear to be woven into a liquid textile (bottom right). The lodge is run on solar power, so all one can hear is the lapping of waves on the beach below and the occasional sounds of alpacas being chased out of the garden.

Out in a small open boat, the waters turn an ominous inky black, but this time the threatening storm keeps its distance (top left). The journey round Suasi takes an hour's gentle rowing.

From the island of Taquile, the southern lake shores are just visible, half an hour after sunset (bottom left). Though well populated, the island has neither electricity nor dogs to disturb the peace.

On the southern tip of Suasi is a hill 450 feet (135m) high; from its top one can see most of the lake, with the earth's curve bending away across the surface and the sunset at eye level. The small hill feels like a mountain while one watches the clouds around the lake's rim drift out over the water (both right).

66

The island of Taquile is run on communal principles, with visitors being assigned to stay with families on a rotational basis. The islanders are an anomaly in that they are Quechua speakers in an Aymara region. Their culture, too, can be seen as a last link to that of the conquering Incas, with parts of their traditional dress and the *mit'a* (shared labour) forming a bond between themselves, and with their ancestors.

The black cloak worn by the women (far left, top) is very similar to those worn in the town of Tinta near Cuzco. From drawings made soon after the conquest, it is clear that this costume was common in Inca times.

One child wears his traditional waistcoat over white shirt and dark trousers, as the other boy and girl await a game of football and volleyball (top left).

Both boys wear the *chullo* (flapped hat) common throughout the Peruvian Andes. The *chullo* protects the ears, but also prevents the chapping of the cheeks, another common sight at this altitude.

The duties of men and women are divided, though they work together on the same task. Here (left), the women take a break with the sacks they use to carry earth, while the men lift the flagstones of the plaza. Note the lake horizon with its small band of clouds.

As the old town hall is torn down (above), men wait in turn to step forward and carry away the stone blocks. The islanders are famous for their fine weavings, especially the Taquile caps worn here; the white-tipped ones signify single status.

The Pucará civilization is considered to be the oldest major Andean culture of the region. The influence of their sunken plazas with zoomorphic heads protruding from the walls is seen at the great temple of Tiahuanaco over the border in Bolivia. Sections of the terraced pyramids here at Pucará itself (left) strongly resemble Lupaca and Inca walls built a thousand years later. Their figurative sculptures (above) include representations of malevolent gods wielding severed heads as well as human figures with wings and claws. The bas-relief pictured here (right) clearly represents a jaguar, with the spotted design from nose to tail. Once again it shows an intimate knowledge of the jungle, from where the earliest peoples to reach South America, some 15–20,000 years ago, first set foot on these highlands. Such intricate and realistic depictions occur in many pre-Inca cultures, in weavings, ceramics and carved stone. The later austere abstractions of the Incas are therefore evidence of a deliberate and dramatic transformation of style.

Cutimbo is a tall *mesa* (table mountain) standing high above the plains southwest of Puno, its cliffs littered with caves containing many hundreds of skeletons and cave paintings. The burial *chullpas* of the Lupaca culture here (top left) are some of the finest examples in existence. A burial urn found buried outside the towers was painted in separate halves; one Lupaca, the other Inca. It contained a skull, presumably someone born of both cultures. The *chullpas* may have been influenced by Inca architecture, but it seems more likely that the masons of Lupaca and Tiahuanaco, themselves influenced by the ancient Pucará civilization, were conquered and taken back to Cuzco where their building style was incorporated into what is thought of as classically Inca. The stepped design incorporated into Sun and Water temples at Ollantaytambo in the Sacred Valley is known to have originated in this area.

A male puma guards the door to the burial chamber (bottom left). Sacred in virtually all American cultures, pumas sit astride the top of all food chains in both northern and southern halves of the continent. They range from the snows of Alaska to the jungles and deserts of South America. Also known as cougar and mountain lion, 'puma' is one of the few Quechua words to have entered the English language.

Zoomorphic figures carved into the *chullpas* are a clear indicator of strong links with the jungle provinces to the east. Whether this pair of animals (far right, top) are bears from the cloud forest or monkeys from the rainforest is debatable.

A large monkey with prehensile tail, probably representing the red howler, Amazonia's noisiest resident (right). It is not known whether this block was part of a fallen *chullpa*, or stood apart.

Tachymenis peruviana, a small rear-fanged snake, is the only species of snake found at such high altitudes in the region (far right, bottom). (Cutimbo stands at nearly 12,650 feet/4,000m.) A herpetologist friend later suggested that I should have pickled it, as a potential new subspecies. Lack of pickle and jar was my excuse for not having done my scientific duty.

The domestication and pastoral herding of animals was the foundation of the earliest Andean civilizations, especially in this region. The grey uniform of a compulsory education and red shirt of a football team are symbols of today's cultural necessities. Sheep arrived with the Spanish, and are encouraged by evangelists as llamas do not appear in the Bible. The llama, impure as it may be, does far less harm to the environment.

The mild microclimates of the Moho and Conima bays provide perfect growing conditions for a wide variety of flowers. It is a delightful surprise to round a bend in the harsh dry landscape at over 13,000 feet (4,000m) and find villages awash with colourful gardens. Dahlias, gladioli and vast vegetables abound, but the old-fashioned roses with their fabulously heavy scents are the unequivocal show stealers.

Pure-blooded Uro natives have disappeared, having intermarried with Aymaras. Uros' descendants continue to live on the traditional floating islands, made of layered reed matting woven 6 feet (1.8m) thick. Their livelihood is now the selling of tourist trinkets rather than fishing, and since the 1960s they have been evangelical Christians. Their tortora-reed vessels (previous page) are of the type used by Thor Heyerdahl on his Kon-Tiki expedition; similar craft are used on the Pacific coast.

Based on the premise that the vast majority of the population are illiterate, for many years political parties have used symbols to advertise themselves. Unusually, these examples (left) in Sicuani and Lampa are pleasing to the eye; political daubings on walls, rocks, cliffs and trees, in fact any dry surface, are as widespread and ugly as the habit of dropping litter.

This whitewashed church near Huancane (bottom right) has the delightfully naïve simplicity of nearly all adobe buildings. The fact that they are made of the earth on which they stand gives them a charm generally lacking in cheap modern architecture.

The abandoned turn-of-the-seventeenth-century church at Tintiri near Putina (top right) is altogether more intricate, and shows what can be done with the humble mud brick. A Peruvian-British family has recently bought this wonderful example of faded Andean baroque, with a view to restoring and protecting it from further decay.

Within the church at Lampa stands a mausoleum to Enrique Torres Bellón, a local politician and benefactor who, having remodelled the main square and church, created this black marble crypt for his everlasting memory (left). Below the dome are some 400 skulls and skeletons in a gruesome *memento mori* spectacle. The skeletons are those of members of the Spanish colonial nobility, giving the display a further salutary twist on death's supremacy.

On top of the dome stands the world's only life-sized replica of Michelangelo's *La Pietà* (above). The loan of a mould from the Vatican enabled this aluminium version to be cast. When the original sculpture in Rome was vandalized in the 1980s, representatives from Italy came to this tiny Andean town to measure up its twin.

In the 'rose-coloured' town of Lampa, Waca-waca dancers in a paint-powdered street display costumes typical of the department of Puno (right). Their origins are a mix of cultural styles including large metal masks copied from the Far East. The relatively recent introduction of miniskirts and athletic routines seem to have been influenced by the Rio carnival, while more traditional Llamerito dance groups representing the herders of the region have all but disappeared. At Mass in Lampa church, the large metal breastplates shining by candlelight (top left) and furry outfit of a devil creature (far right) apparently mesmerized by the Virgin, are further signs of dynamic and adaptable customs.

The ubiquitous bowler hats and multilayered skirts worn by the women of the Puno region are also on the wane, as an older sister chooses baseball cap and sports top to display her progressive good taste (bottom left).

Even in more remote towns such as Moho, where traditions hold firm, the younger members of a crowd watching the town's anniversary celebrations dress like children from Los Angeles or Manchester (above). Around them, the thick cloaks held with long silver clasps and pins date back to well before the conquest; the bowler hats worn by the elder women, however, are a distorted inheritance left by male railway workers from Great Britain at the turn of the twentieth century.

The Sicuri dancers, their hats decorated with dyed grass and feathers, are the more traditional representatives of local culture (left). In the main square of Moho, their rhythmic drum and pipe dances hark back to their Aymara ancestors, stringed instruments having arrived with the Europeans. Seven other dance groups waiting to compete with them appear equally faithful to their heritage, though few realize that their colourfully striped ponchos were first introduced as the drab utilitarian garments of sixteenth-century Spanish peasants. It is typical of Andean culture to have exaggerated and brightened the design.

4 CUZCO

The Navel of the Earth

> Antisuyo to the east, Chinchaysuyo to the north, Contisuyo to the west and Collasuyo to the south. This we conceived standing in Cuzco, which is the centre and capital of all the earth. And my ancestors there in the centre called themselves Lords of Tahuantinsuyo – which is to say, Lords of the Four Parts of the World – for they thought there could surely be no more world than this.
>
> TITU CUSI YUPANQUI INCA *The Relacion, at Vilcabamba*

> I promised them gold … well, they've got gold. The cripples have gold crutches. The coughers spit gold snot. The bargain's over.
>
> PETER SHAFFER'S FRANCISCO PIZARRO *The Royal Hunt of the Sun*

In modern accounts of Cuzco and its history, writers' descriptions are tinged with their sympathies towards the conquerors or the conquered. Even physical descriptions talk in terms of sad stones, or churches built with blood. Of all the people who have written about it, Ernesto 'Che' Guevara grasped the dichotomy with even-handed passion. He describes the different effects of the Cuzcos that he sees. The plaintive city of violated temples, looted palaces and brutalized Indians, inviting you to take up a warrior's club and defend the Inca way of life. The picturesque city of red-tiled harmony, traditional costumes of local colour and narrow streets, inviting you to pick up a camera, the reluctant tourist. And the vibrant city of libraries, museums and decorated churches, monuments to the formidable courage of the soldiers of Spain. This Cuzco invites you to don armour, sit astride a powerful steed, ride out and conquer.

What instantly strikes the modern visitor is the beautiful balanced serenity of the main square. It is strange to sit on a carved wooden balcony overlooking the plaza, sunlight pink on the arched colonnades and church and read about the horrors that took place there.

When more civilized men arrived from Spain they rued their compatriots' zealous greed, recognizing, even in the sixteenth century, the shame to come. The people of the mountains still suffer an anxiety of flux between the two cultures and the sensitive visitor feels a faint discomfort between the beauty and the history. But sometimes still, when you read the stories of the worst abuses, you are struck by an impotent rage. Real anger. I remember showing friends around the remains of a particularly badly damaged temple and a senior British banker stood shaking his head 'I've a couple of Spaniards in my team in London', he said 'd'you think I should dock their Christmas bonus'

The founding of Cuzco is lost in time. The legend of Manco Qapaq's golden staff sinking into the ground is typical of the Incas who retold history to their own glory, absorbing the myths of other nations as they expanded. With no written language, the colonial chronicles, recollections of eyewitnesses and folklore through the complicated bias of both writer and speaker, are the basis of history. Father Cobo, whose seventeenth-century writings tell us much about Cuzco, explained that the term *ñaupapacha* covered all periods 'a long time ago', stretching from twenty years back to a thousand, 'except that when the thing is very ancient, they express this by a certain accent and ponderation of their words'.

Even eminent archaeologists are not in full agreement. John Rowe dates the foundation of Cuzco to around 1240, with a sudden expansion into surrounding lands in 1438. Brian Bauer, however, believes the peaceful amalgamation of local tribes in the area began as early as AD 1100 with the fading of the Killke culture, itself a successor to the Huaris. There are extensive Huari remains very close to Cuzco, and it is possible that some such structure lay on the site of Coricancha, the Inca Sun Temple at the centre of Cuzco. Most agree that around 1438 an attack on Cuzco by the Chanca tribe was repulsed by Pachacuteq, who is thought to have then followed up his unexpected victory with the massive expansion and domination of the continent. John Hemming describes him as an Alexander the Great figure in Andean history. He is believed to have laid the master plans of Tahuantinsuyo, based on divine descent from the Sun and a rigorously ordered society. The austerity of the architecture is symbolic of his efficiency, a deliberate aesthetic of simplicity when compared with the ancient figurative masonry of Pucará and Tiahuanaco to the south.

From Coricancha, centre of the navel, lines known as *ceques* radiated in every direction with 400 sacred rocks, springs, caves and boulder shrines along them. These formed some kind of calendar and *sucaca* towers were built to measure celestial risings and settings, transits and oppositions. R. Tom Zuidema and Brian Bauer have built extensively on the notes of Cobo regarding these lines. The *ceques* include the four lines dividing the world into quarters. As seen in the opening quote, the eastern part or *suyo* was named Anti, after a jungle tribe; this was later corrupted to Andes. (In the same way, 'Peru' was a corruption of Biru, the name of a northern tribe.) A compromise between the solar year of 365¼ days and the lunar year of 354 (12 x 29½ days) was accomplished with a device similar to the modern leap year: a day is inserted before the June solstice every third or fourth year.

The city was laid out in the shape of a puma, with Sacsayhuaman on the hill above forming the head. The rivers Tullumayo and Saphi bordered it on two sides, and a vast double square divided into Aucaypata, the square

of war (or weeping), and Cusipata, the joyful square, was the site of many festivals. The current Plaza de Armas and Plaza Regocijo stand on this site today.

When other civilizations were absorbed, heirs were brought to Cuzco and married into the Inca dynasty. In 1470, Minchancaman, leader of the highly organized coastal Chimu, was married to the Inca's daughter. The same system was used in religion. Within Coricancha stood the famous Punchao, or solar Sun Disc. Icons and idols of conquered tribes were placed there where they continued to be worshipped in a pantheon of pan-Andean religions. Meaning 'Golden Enclosure', the Coricancha included an area of life-sized corn, with a large tree and various animals, all made of gold and silver in the finest detail. They were later melted down into ingots. In *The Conquest of the Incas*, John Hemming relates that when the first three Spaniards arrived to strip the panels from the walls, they also found a tomb with jewel-bedecked mummies. An old lady with a golden mask and armed with a flywhisk demanded that they remove their boots. Having meekly complied, they proceeded to steal precious stones and objects from the tomb.

The majesty of the Inca was extraordinary. Should he wish to spit, one of the chosen women would raise her hand for him to use as a receptacle. His clothes were worn once and then burnt, and the reverence and fear in which he was held astonished the Spaniards. They described Atahualpa's features as noble and were impressed with both his capacity to learn (he played chess very well) and the dignity with which he behaved. The contrast with Cieza de León's description of Diego de Almagro, Pizarro's partner in the conquest, sums up the difference in leadership: 'short stature, with ugly features, but of great courage and endurance . . . it could be said of him that his lineage began and ended with himself.'

After his capture, Atahualpa conceded he had planned to kill most of the conquistadors, retain some as eunuchs and then breed their fabulous horses. The Incas *were* brutal and merciless in many of their campaigns, but comparisons with the Spanish in the morality of warfare are simplistic. What is clear is that in the skill of their engineering, agriculture and architecture, and in the support and care of their subjects, they far surpassed the Europeans. Throughout the empire of Tahuantinsuyo, the legacy of these disparities lives on.

From a high pass above San Jerónimo, Cuzco is a pool of electric light, while the snow peaks of the Urubamba range glow by moonlight beyond the Chinchero plain and the Sacred Valley (previous pages).

Launched from the church of San Cristóbal, fireworks careen over the Plaza de Armas on Cuzco's notional birthday near the June winter solstice (left). The church was built in front of the remains of Colcampata, the palace of the founding Inca, Manco Qapaq. To the right, Christ the Redeemer, a replica of Rio de Janeiro's icon, is illuminated all year.

The earliest rays of dawn striking the eastern flank of Mount Ausangate, seen on the horizon, have a poetic significance as the Sun and Apu were the most powerful gods in their realms (top right). A conjunction of celestial and earthly gods was considered particularly auspicious. In the foreground, the elegant Compañía, church of the Jesuits, dominates the square from the site of the palace of Huayna Qapaq, the last ruler of a united Inca empire.

The large flat cobbles of Cuzco's main square shine with the December rains (bottom right). The Plaza de Armas was once the open ceremonial square of the Incas. It was twice the size in pre-conquest days, and these colonial Spanish buildings on the western side of the square, opposite the cathedral, divide the remains of the original in two. The pillared arches, intricately carved wooden balconies and terracotta roof tiles are typical; in spite of the destruction that brought them into existence, they lend the city a dramatic charm of their own.

The polygonal cyclopean masonry is the Incas' greatest testament to their supremely well-structured society. The stonework of post-conquest masons is obvious, as if their pride in their work had died with their God-King. Nearly all temples and palaces were torn down after Manco Inca's rebellion of 1536. Impatient noblemen used the already dressed stones of Inca structures to build their own. Those walls left standing give an inkling of the grand scale and austere style of imperial Cuzco, but even sixteenth-century Spaniards arriving after the years of war bemoaned the barbarous destructiveness of their compatriots in the preceding 30 years.

Seen through a colonial Spanish doorway (above), a schoolgirl passes the famous Hatun Rumiyoc or 'great stone' after which the street is named. Part of the palace of the Inca Roca, the wall survives on three sides of the building which is now the archbishop's palace. The great stone itself has twelve sides and corners and has become an enduring symbol of Cuzco, appearing on everything from travel brochures to beer bottles.

Four details from the walls of the Inca Roca's palace (bottom left, centre left, top right and centre right). The knobs left jutting from the surface are believed to have been used to attach woven grass ropes when dragging

the stones along on gravel or stone rollers. They were left for some long-forgotten aesthetic effect, possibly incorporating the movement of their shadows. (In the Huarochiri manuscript, an anonymous description of Inca culture, officials who watched and interpreted shadows cast by such gnomons are called Yancas.)

At the Water Temple of Tambo Machay (top left), just outside Cuzco, a right-angled bend in both wall and staircase demonstrates the supreme skill of Inca architects and masons. The Inca style of building is particularly resistant to earthquake damage, with rocks interlocking on three sides.

Different styles of Inca masonry exist at various sites, as can be seen in Chapter 6. In the classic masonry of Cuzco, the two styles are the polygonal-shaped walls and the tiered courses of stone seen in Loreto street (bottom right), the longest surviving Inca wall in Cuzco. It was the former Acllahuasi, 'House of the Chosen Women', and, by a historical twist of fate, now houses the nuns of the order of Santa Catalina.

The sacred watercourse at Tambo Machay (above left) is a fine example of engineering, with an underground duct bringing water from the next hill. There were over 300 temple shrines around Cuzco, the vast majority of which were pulled down or buried. This and several other surviving temples at least provide examples of how things were, though it is likely that trees and plants once enclosed the site and its baths. The trapezoidal niches seen at the top are characteristic of Inca design.

The Compañía, church of the Jesuits, in the Plaza de Armas (above right), is one of the few Spanish buildings that do any kind of justice to the structures that stood before. A project surrounded by great controversy, it was seen as a direct challenge to the supremacy of the rather squat cathedral to its right, but by the time Pope Paul III ruled against further construction it was virtually complete. The fears were well founded; to this day it eclipses its neighbour. In his classic Andean novel *Deep Rivers*, José María Arguedas writes of it:

'Instead of being overpowering, it made me rejoice. I felt like singing in the doorway . . . the Cathedral was too big.' On Sundays, the national and Cuzco flags are raised in the plaza.

An architectural detail in one of the last remaining grand colonial houses not to have fallen down or been restored as a hotel or museum (right). With its combination of noble background, weathered façade and lack of funds, it has the charm of an aged aristocrat fallen on hard times.

The cave and altar at Q'enqo stand at the heart of an intricately carved rock shrine (left). Q'enqo means 'zigzag' in Quechua, and, on the top surface, heavily eroded rock has indeed been carved into zigzagging channels thought to have been used for divination purposes. There are many similar carved channels throughout the region. A liquid, probably a local maize beer called *chicha*, would have been poured down the channels, and the direction taken by the liquid would have been significant. At times blood may have been used, though more likely llama than human. The cave itself is thought to have housed mummies of minor royalty; the mummies of the Incas themselves remained in their palaces, with their retinue of servants and relatives attending them as if they still lived.

The cave entrance to the Temple of the Rainbow is several hours' walk up the Saphi *quebrada* (right). At the winter solstice the sun penetrates the cave at midday, causing a series of rainbows in a temporary waterfall created by a blocked stream above. When standing in the icy waterfall a perfectly circular rainbow appears on the end of your toes. Unfortunately, pseudo-mystics have taken to painting their garish designs on the walls of the cave, spoiling the sacred place for those who follow. Cuzco attracts many people interested in esoteric studies, and their reputation suffers due to the activities of half-baked egocentrics solely interested in exploitation of one kind or another.

In Inca times, as with many more ancient cultures, the winter solstice was the most important festival of the year; with the shortest day past, rebirth and regeneration, and the sowing and harvesting of crops could be anticipated and celebrated. The Sun Festival or Inti Raymi took place on June 21st. In the months preceding this date, on every third or fourth year, an extra day was inserted to keep the calendar working, very much like our leap year.

On the day of Inti Raymi, a chant would begin before dawn, rising in volume as the Sun appeared. Hundreds of people would keep up this reverent sound all day, until after sunset. Many offerings of fine weavings and llamas would have been made and the intensity of the celebrations would have been truly awesome. The Inca would dig the first soil of the season with great ceremony and at times have llamas thrown to the poorest members of the crowd, causing 'great sport' according to the chronicler Cristóbal de Molina.

The festival was soon prohibited by the Spanish, and largely forgotten, until in 1944 a group of Cuzco intellectuals decided to revive the custom. The date June 24th was settled on, and every year a procession with Inca, generals, *ñustas* (princesses) and attendants moves from the Coricancha, the Temple of the Sun in Cuzco's centre, to the fortress of Sacsayhuaman on the hill above.

On the gigantic ramparts of Sacsayhuaman, an audience of some 40,000 watch a cast of local people representing pilgrims of the four *suyos* paying homage. The Inca appears in his litter and is portered to stand astride a central *usnu* platform made of painted card (right). He addresses his people and the Sun in a grave Quechua speech, and various offerings and performances are made in his honour. It is a great spectacle with resourceful costumes and choreography, but so far from the awe-inspiring performance of a God-King, and without the drama of many more genuine festivals, that it cannot help but remain something of a pantomime.

There is no doubt that Sacsayhuaman is one of the most impressive stone monuments left standing in the world. Where Machu Picchu's reputation rests on its dramatic situation and discovery, Sacsayhuaman is sheerly awe-inspiring in its stature and form. With three tiered ramparts of limestone blocks, some over 27 feet (8m) high and weighing over 350 tons, this zigzagged wall stretches along the flat open land, defending the only side otherwise unprotected by the steep slopes descending into the city. The name is thought to mean 'Royal Eagle' though, in his excellent *Exploring Cuzco*, Peter Frost also puts forward the case for a corruption of *sacsa uma*, meaning 'speckled head', which would fit with the theory that Cuzco was originally laid out in the shape of a puma, with Sacsayhuaman representing the head. From above, the outline of the puma does appear to be credible, but the zigzags as teeth goes too far; in any overlaid diagram they rest on the ridge of the brow and nose.

Sacsayhuaman has many interesting foundations upon its various levels. A vast round reservoir was discovered in 1985 and the bases of three enormous towers with intricate watercourses stand on the defended stretch overlooking Cuzco. All of these were torn down by stone-hungry conquistadors, too impatient to wait for newly quarried blocks. Though not solely a fortress, it is in this role that its most dramatic moments are recorded – specifically in May 1536, when Manco Inca's rebellion very nearly dislodged the invaders. Having been trapped within a building in the town below, the Spaniards, with characteristic valour, rode out and up to the north of Sacsayhuaman; reeling right they took Rodadero Hill, upon which the carved steps of the so-called Inca Throne (left) and the natural formation used as a slide for many generations (top right) appear. In this position across the flat area from the zigzagged ramparts they battled for two days, during which Juan Pizarro, the leader's half-brother, was slain by slingshot. Eventually they took the main buildings with scaling ladders. The battle is described in great detail in John Hemming's *The Conquest of the Incas*, in which individual acts of bravery and the overall strategies and desperation of those days leap off the page.

In the graveyard at Huancaro, the children's section is particularly moving, with parental grief clearly seen in the loving attention paid to the tiny graves (top left). The dates painted on the back name days in the near future. Talking to the young grave-diggers, they turn out to be due dates for the annual rent of plots; non-payment results in abrupt disinterment. Nearly all the holes being dug are for bodies coming out, like so many Yoricks, not going in. They are unceremoniously dumped on a slope with tattered plastic flowers, rotten plywood and the odd shoe. Suddenly, the kitsch pink metal takes on an altogether more profound significance.

Three old gentlemen of Cuzco, their style of dress a common sight on the streets, but only for as long as their generation endures (bottom left). The black-and-white portraits of the twentieth-century master photographer Martín Chambi captured these men in their youth, but like so many costumes once worn in the surrounding mountains and jungles, they will soon be a two-dimensional record only. In a fateful twist, the man on the left passed the café where I was writing these captions; I rushed out to show him this portrait of him and his friends taken some six years earlier. Nodding gently, he corrected me: 'Those are not friends of mine, but brothers, with a cousin in between; yes, they still live, but I am not in this picture, we are alike, and sometimes mistaken . . .'

A startlingly realistic statue of Santa Rosa of Lima, in the church of Santo Domingo (right). The church stands on top of the Coricancha, Temple of the Sun, the most sacred centre of the Inca empire, the navel of the navel. Recent sonar readings and excavations below the altar suggest that Inca tunnels and crypts, centuries lost, lie below. Evidence suggesting that the Huari tribe may have placed their temple on the same spot, long before the Incas, has also been found. In an annual dust-down, the leathery hands of an elderly lady remove the layers of flowers, vestments and the Christ-child from the icon of the coastal capital of the invaders.

The discordant sounds of brass bands competing with each other and within themselves become a marvellous tune of their own over the terracotta roofs. There are many such noisy festivals, with fireworks tossed carelessly into the air. Here, it is Corpus Christi; 40 men struggle under the weight of San Sebastián (far right), as their fathers did before them. Pierced with arrows he is a pitiful sight, but as with the blood-spattered representations of Christ in every church, these people must have icons who have suffered more than they, and that takes all the gory tricks of an artisan's trade. In Inca times, the mummies of the 12 Incas were paraded around the old square; now it is 12 saints. Adapting and absorbing cultural symbols has been the Quechua way for nearly 1,000 years – the early peaceful conquests of neighbouring tribes included the placing of their most sacred objects in the Coricancha Temple of the Sun, and the Virgin Mary is still closely identified with Pacha Mama (Mother Earth). The very latest icon that year, a Pokémon Pikachu, appears on a balloon held on the robes of Santiago the Moor-Killer (bottom left). Faith is displayed in potent acts of reverence, penitence and humility, while sacristans feed ice-lollies to choirboys (bottom right) and policemen read sheet-music pegged to the back of the man in front (top right).

Easter Monday is the feast-day of Cuzco's patron, El Señor de los Temblores, Lord of the Earthquakes. Each year he is festooned with the scarlet petals of the Nuc'chu flower in the cathedral (top left), and brought out on to the streets, which are also covered with the blossom. More are thrown by townspeople from the pavements and balconies along his winding route through Cuzco. Some devotees say his mysteriously dark appearance comes from the pigment in the petals. Seen here in the first church visited, Santa Teresa (right), his robes are changed by major-domos (below left), members of Cuzco's senior families who accompany him from cathedral to every major church and back. Cuzco's last major earthquake was in 1950, though a tremor also did considerable damage in 1986.

Christ the Redeemer stands within a fence, away from graffiti-scrawling hands (top left). He was a gift from grateful Palestinian refugees in 1949 and overlooks the centre of Cuzco from the horizon alongside Sacsayhuaman. Along the road, at Puca Pucara, is yet another symbol of cultural adaptation as the native knitters of Cuzco turn their hands to the designs of distant Aran (bottom left); this is a deal better than the nineteenth-century practice of sending wool to the mills of northern England then buying back the factory-woven cloth.

Andean security from both town and country. The earthen adobe walls and use of lowly materials betray a rustic ingenuity. The broken bottles in San Blas are harsher yet resourceful too. Both systems appear to work and both are in stark contrast to the cement enclosures and electrified fences of those with more to lose. In Tahuantinsuyo theft was virtually unknown and punishable by stoning. The Spanish conquest was an orgy of theft from beginning to end.

5 THE SACRED VALLEY

Earthly Paradise

We left the Pisac market … and travelled … under long avenues
of eucalyptus … in this loveliest of all valleys I have ever seen.
PETER MATTHIESSEN *The Cloud Forest*

Nothing obtains the good will of an Indian sooner than his being
requested to spare a little coca. He pulls out his pouch with an air
of utmost satisfaction, and seems anxious to have it supposed that
he feels the honour most sensibly.
GENERAL MILLER, COMMANDER BRITISH VOLUNTEER FORCE, 1824

To the native Runa, the landscape is a living thing filled
with guardian deities. The *Tirakuna*, 'those who watch
over us', are perceived in every notable feature. In caves,
springs, lakes and boulders, benevolent or capricious
spirits watch over all aspects of their lives like elder
members of a community. Each landmark has a name
and a distinct personality, some combined with Auccis,
the spirits of distant ancestors. Leaves of the sacred coca
bush are left for them in offerings of reverence.

Coca is used as a medium to communicate with
Pacha Mama (Mother Earth) and the array of local gods.
In these offerings, and in the reciprocal sharing and
chewing of the leaves, the community is bonded
together. The giving and receiving of coca is the opening
of any social encounter. '*Hallpakusunchis*', they greet one
another, 'Let us chew coca together'. It is also a
medicinal tonic with magical powers, and is used for
reading the future or as a payment to earth spirits for
special requests. It is also chewed for the alkaloids
released that can quell hunger and the effects of *soroche*
(altitude sickness). When tourists fly straight into Cuzco
from the coast they are offered coca tea to help them
adjust. There is a vast distinction between the leaf and

chemically processed cocaine, and the effect of the tea is
weaker than that of a cup of espresso. (Coca-Cola began
as a chilled version.) In Inca times, it is thought, the
chewing of the leaf was permitted only in the highest
echelons of society. Bales of the best leaves, some grown
especially for the purpose, were burnt as offerings.

In Cuzco, the Sacred Valley of the Incas is known
simply as 'The Valley'; one can see its name on a
hundred signs, advertising river rafting, pony trekking,
mountain biking and a list of ruins to tick off before
tea. In short, a destination. But the beaten track is
narrow, and the large tour groups never leave it; their
only impact is on the major ruins in the heat of the day.
When the sites are looking their finest, at dawn, dusk
or in moonlight, the vast majority are in their hotels
and restaurants, eating and sleeping. Those who love it
come back by themselves, taking in their favourite spots
at a calmer pace.

The roads to the valley from Cuzco climb high
before dropping. Each time, the landscape differs,
altered by crops and seasons, emerald through to myriad
dry browns. The light will touch a different hill, or bend
in the river and catch your eye as new. Scents on the

currents of warm air are equally atmospheric: of yellow broom in bloom, eucalyptus woodsmoke and leaves, and the faint reek of a skunk startled and gone.

Driving over the plains of Chinchero and Maras one reaches the point where the flat-bottomed valley stretches out in either direction far below. In front stands the dramatic peak of San Juan, with the Chicon glacier alongside it. Between the deep greens of the valley and the frigid high ice lie spectacular vertical ridges and folds, dry brown, scarred in deep sculpted shadow accentuating the day's end. The peaks of the Urubamba range sweep away left and right. Sawasiray and Helancoma, Media Luna and the pyramidic Veronica/Huacay Huilca. Finally, the descent begins down long switchbacked hairpin bends. At night the electric-orange street grid of Urubamba lights up, toy bright in the darkness.

Each little town is a beacon of square lines of light. It is odd to think that just fifteen years ago all of them were candle-lit, with gas lamps and the smell of kerosene. The arrival of television brought crowds around the doorways of the restaurants that owned them. One link controlled all the sets in the valley. Whatever the man with the mast watched, so did the valley's inhabitants. During the World Cup semi-finals of 1986 he made the grave error of switching to a soap opera. Three carloads of men screeched to a halt outside his house. Several plot lines came and went before the soap opera was shown again, following a less violent protest by the wives.

Outside the archaeological towns, with their wonderful teeming markets, the valley is like a giant farm, old-fashioned and bucolic. The teams of oxen towing wooden *yuntas* (ploughs) plod back and forth, year in year out, slicing the earth into rumpled furrows. Field by field, they darken the valley floor like a screen-saver. Small mixed herds are shooed along tracks and roads at the end of the day. Several donkeys laden high, sheep bedraggled in unison, a cow, a sow and a couple of piglets, short blurred legs running to keep up.

Lives, as in the days of the Inca, are punctuated by festivals, often ancient with Christian overtones. The Incas called November *Aya Marca Killa*, 'the moon [month] when we carry the dead'. November 2nd is the Day of the Dead, when graveyards come alive. Plants and flowers are placed and planted, replacing the old or joining them. Stones are scrubbed and tombs repainted.

Some bring portraits. All bring booze, and a merry inebriation settles over the afternoon. Huddles of heads in circles and lines nod and smile in recollection. Children scurry, shrieking with laughter, chasing each other round the graves of friends and relatives alive again in stories. Bones are dusted off, and placed somewhere safe. Loud mirth and quiet anguish surge and falter in turn. Cups are filled and spilled on the ground for Pacha Mama and on to headstones for the dead to drink. The day draws on. The stories get longer and laughter louder. Silences open and close. As the light fails behind the peaks the raucousness recedes. Men stagger out to relieve themselves against the graveyard wall, while others snore through geraniums, arms wrapped round stone. A grandmother's skull adorned with a ribbon is cradled by a gently weeping man. He misses her and wants to take her home. It seems a good idea to everyone and he wipes his nose and smiles. Later, in the chilled darkness, drunks awake and leave with a flourish of goodbyes.

Next day by contrast there is a child's first haircut. The *Rutuchico* involves friends and relatives each cutting a lock in turn and placing it wrapped round a gift of money on a large plate. The child is only one or two; too young to understand. But older brothers and sisters revel in the ceremony of it within their own house: the sprinkled petals, clip of scissors, growing stack of hair and notes and their sibling's newly spiky head. The ritual took place in Inca times, presumably with gifts of food and crafted toys. As bottles of beer are opened, guinea pigs roam the kitchen floor, whistling their clumsy chorus, blissfully unaware of where their mates have gone and what we shall have for lunch.

Up and down the valley, people work the fields again with sore heads and quieter jokes. The salt pans of Maras twinkle in the sunlight, hummingbirds flit around a ruined mill, high on the cliffs, ancient painted figures of llamas and herders are partly hidden by overhanging moss. Clay graves, long since pillaged, stand gaping. In stormy weather condors wheel down from the heights; today the rains have still not come. Not a cloud or a condor in sight.

The close proximity of diverse habitats is illustrated by the view from the damp Polylepis forest of Yanacocha (Black Lake) to the fertile floor of the Sacred Valley (previous pages). The valley walls display the arid highland environment of cactus and aloe. It was the warm tropical fertility of the valley, only a short distance from Cuzco and yet a climatic world away, that made it sacred. Living in a city way above the tree line, the Incas were still able to consume the luxurious fresh produce of tropical vegetables, fruit and the sacred coca leaf.

The Gallo-Ttippi, a Spanish-Quechua term meaning literally 'rooster-break', persists today under more politically correct circumstances (top left). Where an unfortunate bird used to hang upside down until pulled in half by the neck, twenty-first-century horsemen reach up for a bouncing bottle of pisco, a grape-based spirit similar to grappa. The cowboys don't mind a bit, saying it is much more pleasant than the gush of warm blood of olden days.

At Pentecost, a variety of masked and costumed groups carry out ritual dances in towns throughout the region. Here Chilenos, a satirical troupe harking back to the war with Chile, hoist a Maqta up a tree to be berated by a stern lawyer wearing a top hat and enormously long-nosed mask complete with black boil at its tip (bottom left). Symbolizing the power of the cruel *hacendado* over the landless peasant, the butt of their humour has evolved over the years from the Chileans to the poor masked Quechua and the overbearing, book-bashing lawyer, an easily recognized and hated figure.

In a friendly continuation of the *mit'a* (the conscripted labour provided in Inca times), fellow villagers help raise the adobe mud bricks, clay tiles and tree trunks needed to construct a house (top right). Favours are returned in the fields or similar constructions. Adobe is the perfect building material in the Andes; cheap, flexible in earth tremors and a great leveller of extreme exterior temperatures, storing heat in the day and releasing it in the chilled nights. The 500-year-old mud storehouse ruins seen on the mountain behind are evidence of adobe's longevity; the symbolic status of an expensive and unsuitable cement house, however, is on the rise.

The long braids, straw and plaster hats, layered skirts and bundled *mantas* (brightly woven blankets) containing babies or goods are almost a uniform for the ladies of Ollantaytambo, seen here eagerly awaiting the results of the annual maize contest (bottom right). Having originated in Mexico, the maize (or corn) crop has been a staple in Peru since pre-Inca times. Its incarnations in this festival include soups, cakes, purée and pizzas.

Andean bullfights are one of the most harrowing events known to man (top left). I have witnessed failed attempts at a clean kill leading to a six-man scrum and the application of a bow-saw. On these occasions the bullfighters were justly if lightly stoned by the crowd. Thankfully a dead bull is beyond the budget of the most remote rings and they are merely toyed with. This bull lived to fight another day, though its shocked expression every time the cape disappeared had us worried for a while.

Donkeys and mules are thoroughly dependable and have taken over from the llama as the pack animal of choice (bottom left). They sometimes find high altitude difficult and occasionally fall off cliffs, but their strength and response to a well-aimed rock are a joy to their handlers, whose limited awareness of animal rights doesn't lead to outright abuse. The two specimens in the background were confused as to whether they were going to appear in the picture or not.

'In the Andes is a little rodent, called a cuy [far right, top]. We call it a guinea pig although it never came from Guinea and is not a pig. Discovering that it was very palatable, the Incas domesticated it and developed a dozen varieties so tame that they can be trusted to run about the floor of an Indian's cabin making no effort to escape and are ready to be caught, killed, cooked and served as a delicious morsel whenever company appears unexpectedly.' So wrote Hiram Bingham, discoverer of Machu Picchu.

The meat of the cuy is not only palatable but contains less than a third of the fat of and 50 per cent more protein than pork, beef and lamb. Guinea pig meat tastes a little like the pink meat of turkey leg. Filled with delicious herb stuffing, they are served whole, fresh from the oven (bottom right). Some varieties grow as big as rabbits. Andean healers pass them over the bodies of the sick and read the entrails to give a diagnosis. Other cuy take the malady on themselves in the process, curing the afflicted by their spontaneous deaths.

This rare article of folk-art (top right) was revealed to me during a festival. A musician placed the little condor-man, made of cuy jaws and ribs, on the inclined surface of his harp. Tapping his fingers on the wood (in the background) the tiny figure staggered forwards, appearing to wave his hands from side to side in minuscule vibrating steps.

The fertility of the land and the warm climate ensure that all manner of plants grow in the Sacred Valley. Here in the garden at the Albergue in Ollantaytambo one finds peaches, avocados, sweet tree-tomatoes, cherries, pears, passion-flowers, all manner of orchids and a giant palm tree, as well as this ginger plant covered in morning dew (above left).

At Urco, between Calca and Yucay, stands a rock shrine with a carved offertory canal wrapped more than 20 feet (6m) around it. At its end is this snake's head, which under the right conditions spits water in a tongue-like fork (above right). The temple may have been used for divining the future or the likely outcome of specific events. It may also have been a site for bathing in sacred pools. Water temples were not unusual in Tahuantinsuyo; when Francisco Pizarro's men first encountered the Inca Atahualpa, he had been bathing at such a place near Cajamarca. It was noted that there were two small canals entering the baths, one cold, the other fed by thermal hot springs, with attendants adjusting the temperature as required. In situations without naturally heated water, pre-heated rocks were placed in streams above the baths. Figurative carvings are usually only found at shrines, the Incas preferring the austere abstraction of lines in their buildings.

A payment of coca for the success of this book is prepared by a *curandero* (above left). As noted by Catherine J. Allen, the gifted anthropologist, 'Coca is the medium of communication with powerful and unpredictable earth deities on and among whom they [the Runa] live.' A lexicon of Quechua terms refers to its qualities and uses. *K'intu* is a small offering of several chosen leaves, *phukuy* is the act of blowing on them, usually in the direction of the nearest Apu and the four winds. *Hallpakusunchis* is an invitation, 'Let us chew coca together'; to refuse is considered a grave insult. Significantly, the name comes from an Aymara word *khoka*, meaning 'the tree', yet another example of the Titicaca region as origin.

As in Inca times, ancestors are included in all festivals. In Ollantaytambo, heirloom skulls are sprinkled with the same yellow confetti of New Year celebrations as the living members of the family (above right). A portrait of Christ and a gift-bearing *ekeko*, for luck, also live in the same Inca niche.

These pictures reflect the profound satisfaction to be found in purity of texture and form. Were it possible, this book would consist of little else.

The carved cliff throne (bottom right) and Sun Temple façade (bottom left) are found in Ollantaytambo.

The people of the Sacred Valley, like their highland relatives, have a deep love of colour with which they surround themselves against a background of browns and greens.

A widow searches for her husband's grave (far left, top). The new high-rise concrete tombs have disorientated her in a graveyard she has known all her life. The origins of the white-plastered top hats worn by women are unclear.

Though the headwear of *chullo* and trilby are a mix of Andean and Spanish, the profile and shape of this man's face (top left) display the pure-blooded features of a true Runa, the name which the Quechua-speaking people call themselves. Among Quechua speakers, the language is called Runasimi.

A young girl expresses her glee at the gift of gladioli (bottom left). She had fetched a pick from her house to help dig out a bogged-down vehicle, so one of the passengers on the way to a wedding gave her the flowers. Reciprocity is the basis on which Andean culture thrives.

At 81, Don Timoteo is one of the oldest inhabitants of the valley, his Spanish features displaying his mixed roots. Pouring a little beer on the ground for Pacha Mama (Mother Earth) as is customary, he murmurs her name before taking a drink himself (far left, bottom).

Children are given responsibilities early in life whether they are caring for younger siblings, the family's livestock or both (above). Education is compulsory and in recent years schools have been built in even the most remote areas. Staffing them is a tougher proposition.

A truck prepares to drive local Runa back to the highland villages above Ollantaytambo (overleaf). This group from the Patacancha valley are easily recognized by their red costumes, which are also worn by the men when working as porters on the Inca Trail to Machu Picchu. The communities, known as *ayllus*, elect a mayor each year known as the Varayoc, for the *vara* or ceremonial silver-tipped staff that is his badge of office.

Young women from Patacancha watching a dance group at the Centro Bartolomé de las Casas (top left). This institution is named after a sixteenth-century Spanish bishop who fought tirelessly for the rights and improved living conditions of the Runa. The centre has three buildings including a College of Andean Studies for students and post-graduates, a library and printing house, and the Casa Campesina, providing cheap accommodation.

At Carnival in February, as with any festival, the Runa women of Huilloc festoon their hats with flowers (below left). The designs on the ponchos include condors, stylized coca leaves and two people on horseback. The poncho was originally introduced as a plain proletarian garment from medieval Spain.

The festival of Carnival in February includes the Day of the Compadres. A man who is godfather to your child is your compadre. Traditionally, all the young men of the region would gather and run from house to house around the communities of their valleys (right), in a ritual that rekindled bonds and drew a line around their territory like the ancient beating of boundaries in Europe. They wore long white sheets on their arms and conch shells were blown as they danced the *Huallata*, representing the Andean goose. This photograph taken in 1989 shows 43 young men receiving tea and soup, the reciprocity of gifts, favours and friendship being at the core of their culture. Mormon missionaries have since entered the area preaching beliefs that prohibit the songs, dances, rituals and alcohol that are intrinsic to the regional festivals. Since the late 1990s, fewer than eight men continue the tradition.

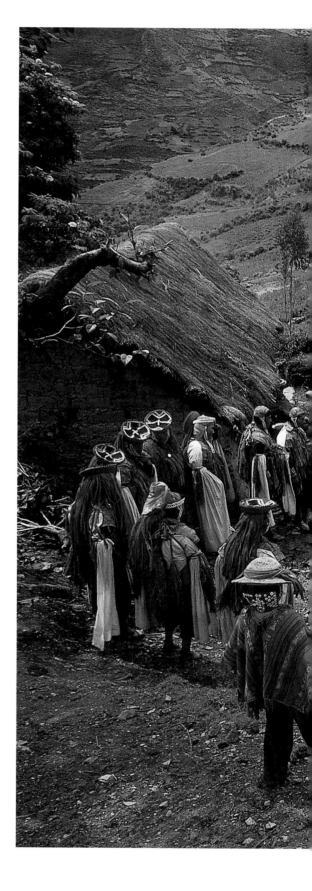

Two entire hillsides at Pisaq (far left, top) have been hewn into vast swathes of terraces, each with its own irrigation canal. On their own, they are extremely impressive, but with the high quality stonework of temples and fortified buildings including an Intihuatana (Hitching Post of the Sun, similar to one at Machu Picchu, see Chapter 7) and a tomb-encrusted cliff, this is one of the most varied and satisfying sites to visit. The views up and down the Sacred Valley are breathtaking, and include the 2-mile (3.3km) stretch of river canalized by the Incas with large retaining walls, the largest pre-Columbian canal in the Americas. Pisaq was possibly named after a local partridge.

Ollantaytambo, in the other three pictures, is the most perfectly preserved Inca town left standing. Laid out on its original grid, with fast-flowing canals running along the streets, many of the buildings remain unchanged apart from the clay roof tiles in place of thatch. A complete study of every building and stone has been carried out by Dr Jean Pierre Protzen of Berkeley, California. This archaeological jewel, almost a living museum, is currently under threat from a large road project leading down to the jungle town of Quillabamba.

The adobe storehouses on Pinkulluna (Hill of Flutes) have survived over 500 rainy seasons due to a sun-baked clay surface (far left, bottom). They were thought to have been prisons for many years, but the lack of internal niches and waterways backed up by descriptions from the chronicles describing storage houses as being situated in high ventilated places, with higher openings at the back where produce was poured in, convinced local historian Robert Randall and Jean Pierre Protzen otherwise. Between the two main buildings some see a king-like head in profile looking left, crowned with a hut and called the Tuñupa. Shapes are seen in every direction, but with no signs of masonry or carving, most of them are spurious.

When Hernando Pizarro's men arrived at the fortress of Ollantaytambo (above) to put down the rebellion of Manco Inca, they received a shock. 'We found it so well fortified that it was a horrifying sight,' quotes John Hemming's *The Conquest of the Incas*. It was the only major siege lost by the Spanish, Manco having flooded the battleground to disable the horses. The Inca himself was seen high on the terraces, in Spanish armour on a captured horse, encouraging his men as Chuncho archers from the rainforest rained arrows on the invaders. Manco was reported to have been greatly depressed by Hernando Pizarro's subsequent overnight retreat, as he knew that the following morning he would have finished them.

The extraordinary salt pans of Maras have been constantly productive since Inca times, and possibly earlier (previous pages). Saline water flows out of the hillside into shallow baths, where it dries by evaporation. The control of water, harvest of salt and final porterage to the road are laboriously carried out by hand. Until recently, many of the workers from the cliff cave town of Pichingoto suffered from goitres, a swelling of the thyroid gland in the neck due to lack of iodine. The mineral is now added in the processing.

A Spanish-style arch greets visitors to the hacienda of Huayo Ccari, or Hanged Man (top left). Situated on high ground above the valley floor, between Yucay and Calca, the gardens and museum offer stunning views. The working farm of the Lambarri Orihuela family also gives a rare insight into life before the Agrarian Reform of 1968.

In the church of Chinchero, a butterfly flies in endless circles on the minute hand of a 'High Class Quartz Clock' (bottom left). Its red flowers are perhaps intended to complement those painted on the original seventeenth-century mural to which it has been nailed.

Pilgrims in the church of Urquillos celebrate the feast of San Juan Bautista, St John the Baptist (top right). The molten wax is collected by some and made into symbolic requests which are stuck on the walls. Naïve drawings of trucks and houses and other desires cover the lower pillars and parapets in the flickering light.

After the Day of the Dead, with the last revellers staggering home, peace returns to the graveyards (bottom right). Tin cans and plastic Inca Kola bottles stand fashioned into vases, the tiny dark letters spelling 'non returnable'. Warm evening wind from the jungle blows dust against freshly painted tombs, rustles through flowers and paper streamers and bends blue the flames of any dying candles left outside.

6 BEYOND THE HILLS

The Remote Outposts

Later, as we stood above a panorama of heart-lifting splendour we counted eight distinct shades of mountain blue … One never becomes used to the Andes; a sense of wonder suffuses every hour.
DERVLA MURPHY *Eight Feet in the Andes*

As the truck lurched, John groaned.
'To me this is hell,' he said.
I stood at the front with the wind in my face. To me it was paradise.
MATTHEW PARRIS *Inca Kola*

By the time you come to read this essay, it is likely that you will have flicked through the whole book and seen its extraordinary range of locations. Imagine that you had the magical power to go to any one of those places now, to close the book, pack a few things and go. These are the choices at hand in Cuzco. You may decide to see a ruin, a fiesta, or even a view, maybe an old favourite or one never seen before, a trail or a hamlet passed a hundred times and never entered. This chapter is filled with those distant places that don't fall into a given geographical category. They are gem-like details; things friends have led me to on overnight trips or week-long tours of exploration. People with a little time on their hands stay in Peru longer than they meant to. Such things as these are the reason why.

On the descent to the jungle or coast, or deep into the interior of Apurimac province, one passes small treasures of colonial towns. Paucartambo is one, on the road to the rainforest of Manu. Sleepy for most of the year, its proverbial one horse is tethered to a palm tree, whisking its tail at flies. Carved wooden balconies and terracotta roofs bend under aged dust, lopsided by time. Cobbles shine after centuries of feet on the winding

streets. The surrounding landscape is a dusty Brueghel, with its feudal hayricks and piles of hand-picked vegetables, irregular-shaped fields on forbidding slopes, cairns of discarded stones and men stooped in manual labour.

At festival times you cannot move for people. A ritual chaos reigns as social anxiety is let loose in a maelstrom of alcohol, fireworks and dance. Rough mock battles of Colla, the Incas' southern foe from Titicaca, and Wayri Chuncho, the jungle allies of the Incas, reel around the town. Oranges, beer and fireworks are fired erupting into the crowds. Troupes gather around the graves of past dancers. Tears are shed, heritage remembered, and the Virgin of Carmen, an Andean mix of the Mother of Christ and Mother Earth, Pacha Mama, comes out of the church to restore order, bringing the cosmos back into harmony until next year.

The Quechua names of these towns have a poetry even before you learn anything else about them: Chinchaypuquio, Livitaca, Coasa, Tarahuasi, Cuyocuyo and Izcuchaca. You arrive and are struck by their individuality, in panorama and detail: an avenue of pisonay (flame trees) 400 years thick, a fountain of mermaids, and unkempt children flicking gravel at the crumpled figure of a sleeping drunk. On the worn steps of the church or in a dark cantina one picks up local tales told with pride. Often there is some emblematic feature for which the town is renowned. Cocharcas, for its eccentric stone church; Mollepata and Tinqui, gateways to the snow peaks; Huarocondo, a sacred cave; Andahuaylillas, fine murals; Curahuasi, for its anis; and the exquisite weavings of Pitumarca.

The faces of the people, and their names, tell silent stories too. The surnames of both parents are carried through life, so family histories of renown or disgrace are as permanent as blood. Even beyond the grave, passers-by may nod or tut at the painted names. Among these pages is a man who lived and died as Visitación Palacio Villegas. There is a lyricism to these titles that is obvious when spoken aloud, or called out across a field. Men are christened José María (Joseph and Mary), Inocencio, Santos, Primitivo or Saturnino. A woman I know is simply Buena Fortuna. And then there is the girl called Madday Innoossa. When her mother was asked what it meant, she walked over to a box of ragged toys, bent down, and pulled out a well-worn, well-loved doll. On its leg, in raised letters, were the words 'MADE IN USA'.

After chatting for a little and hearing that you live there, hidden worlds of private lives open up. A taxi driver once asked if I was interested in artefacts. After a longish journey, he took me into a small storeroom. From inside a leather chest he pulled out several balls of cloth, unravelling them gently to reveal five skulls, of a type I had seen only in museums on the coast. Two of them were elongated like rugby balls, due to tight binding when the person had been a child. Three had the square chipped holes of trepanation – an early forerunner of paracetamol. They were beautiful in a macabre way, and their presentation like something from the X-Files or Indiana Jones. Sadly, skulls are one of the few things on earth I don't collect. I told him I couldn't buy them. He shook his head sadly, 'I thought not maybe, but that you would be enchanted to see them. No?' '¡Encantado completamente!' I answered, and he smiled proudly as he wrapped them up again. He had obviously had them for some time. Though flattered by his trust, and pleased to have seen them, there is something wretched about older people having to sell family treasures.

The humour and wit of the Runa can be subtle, but for the most part it is ribald in the extreme. Many have reminded me of Chaucer's Wife of Bath, as insults are traded in joyfully competitive banter. On a jolting truck journey, a verbal tennis match of comparisons between the opponents' genitalia and that of a wide range of fauna brings tears of mirth. 'Donkey balls' is a clear favourite. Ronald Wright in Cut Stones and Crossroads describes a conversational opening on a similar truck: '"Teach us some English insults", say the girls. I keep the selection as clean as possible, thinking the mother will not appreciate anything too risqué, but when I translate she says: "Hasn't English got anything stronger?"' The humour gets physical when other trucks are passed, as fruit and vegetable skins are hurled with grins as they go by. It is all very warm, open and funny; an intimacy that especially moves me as a lone outsider. The fact that a misti, or white, has bothered to learn any Runasimi, as Quechua calls itself, goes a very long way. The racism of the elite and the snobbery of the mixed-race 'mestizo' middle class often make its speakers feel socially inferior. This is brilliantly portrayed in José María Arguedas' classic novel Deep Rivers. One of the great Latin American writers, Arguedas was himself caught between the two cultures, an uneven struggle that eventually drove him to suicide. To hear some of their beloved words from the mouth of a misti brings emotional responses that, in their very pleasure, reveal the frustrations beneath.

Speaking to travellers who arrive in Cuzco from year-long odysseys around Latin America, it is notable how often Nicaragua and Peru are singled out for the grace and warmth of their people. When climbing the Vilcabamba range, Patrick Leigh Fermor noted their 'grave good manners', and Joe Simpson, in Touching the Void, described the mountain children thus: 'They had a wild, abandoned look about them . . . Everything was done with laughter at an unhurried pace.' For me, an archetypal moment appears in Peter Matthiessen's The Cloud Forest, which captures this very same Inca region in 1961: 'I could not open the window in time to give money to a blind beggar. The pretty Indian child leading her, shuffling along underneath the window as the train drew out of the station, smiled a forlorn smile of understanding. The little girl stopped at last and waved, and the wave stayed with me all the rest of that long day.'

This road descending into the Apurimac canyon has 22 switchbacks (left). The terrain is typical of the department of Apurimac: high plains and *puna* dissected by sheer cliffs and river chasms feeding into the Amazon basin. Impenetrable except by the few dirt roads, it remains one of the most undeveloped and remote places in all Peru. It is consequently full of wonderful surprises.

Built as a bridge, dam, road and canal, this structure above the ruins of Tipón continues up the mountainside until the canal mysteriously ends without a source (top right). It is thought that the snowline used to end here, and that at the time of the conquest a climatic change caused a retreat.

Three canals and waterfalls run alongside the terraces, fields and buildings of Tipón (bottom right). The entire site is irrigated by cut stone channels, displaying engineering skills admirable even by modern standards. The eccentrically shaped fields beyond show that all available land is still cultivated.

An eighteenth-century colonial Spanish balcony, on the verge of collapse (left). It had remained upright in this tenuous manner for many years when it finally fell in 1994. I have a copy framed on my wall and often wonder what has become of Yvetta and her family.

Beyond the fiesta (right). The cochineal-dyed poncho and mountain boots suggest a person of some means and perhaps culture, but three days of dancing and drinking, with little time to sleep, finally take their toll on the best of us. The peel on the ground is left over after a huge orange battle, where the fruit are fired with slings at anyone and everyone.

A group of children pose in front of a remote and ruined church, part of a hacienda left to rot after the land reforms (left). The taking of a photograph is a grave matter for them, their only experience of it being for authoritarian purposes like identification cards. A girl in pink clasps hands as if in prayer; she is conscious of where she stands, roofless or not.

The balustrades in front of this enchanting church rise up over four tall terraces and stretch out for almost 100 feet (30m) on either side (right). It is like an extravagant musical film set, and even more bizarre due to being tucked away in a quiet square at the back end of Sicuani, a little town I had driven past many times before being taken there by a fellow photographer.

Having seen a storm brewing to the south, I set up my tripod for a distant frontal view, 260 feet (80m) across, with people like ants in the windswept concrete foreground. While waiting for the sky to darken behind the church, this little scene off to the side became more and more engaging. A persistent lamb repeatedly interrupted its owner's lunch; butting, nudging and twice leaping right over the bundles into their food. Each time it was calmly rebuffed, and I was drawn in.

To find such a place is fortunate; the added luck of good light and dramatic skies, and finally an occurrence involving someone dressed in the same colour as the scene is extraordinary, and has me grinning till my cheeks ache. I prefer not to use filters or flash, and I don't like posing people, so I depend on this kind of luck, but can still hardly believe it when it happens. Here the lamb finally receives a gentle slap on the nose.

In the main square of Cajamarca, looking for a pretext to launch an attack, a priest gave the Inca Atahualpa, Son of the Sun, a holy book as a representation of the Christian God. Never having seen writing, the God-King tossed it to the ground, unleashing the slaughter of 7,000 of his attendants and soldiers, his own capture and the beginning of the end of the empire. That moment began an ambivalent relationship between the native Peruvians and the Catholic Church which lasts to this day.

On seeing the town church three blocks away, an old lady (left) removes her hat, mutters prayers and weeps for many minutes. Bowing and shuffling her feet, her respect, fear and faith seem to belong to an earlier age when the murals of hell were painted on the walls of Huaro church (far right, bottom).

A more sympathetic painting, of the Cuzco school, has Jesus and his disciples about to dine on cuy (guinea pig) at the Last Supper (top right). Temporarily moved from its usual position in the cathedral, it is seen here during a period of much-needed restoration.

The early Christians tried to crush native beliefs. They destroyed shrines, smashed stone effigies, buried sacred baths and oversaw the melting of the gold from all the temples. ('Do you eat gold?' asks an Inca in a sixteenth-century drawing – it held only sacred value for them, belonging to the Sun.) The Christians' actions are symbolized in a small detail from an oil painting in Chinchero church (far right, top), two angels cutting an Apu (mountain god) in half.

Still the old ways endure. On a grave, flowers are painted for when the real ones die, and a small rock totem is placed carefully under a cross that may also flake away in time (bottom right).

On the streets of the tranquil town of Andahuaylas, an old man observes the vegetables on a market stand, while the yells, helicopters and machine-gun fire of a film blast out of the door behind him.

This statue of General Velasco is the only one I have ever seen. Reviled for his idealistic but disastrous redistribution of land in the 1968 Agrarian Reform, he is a hero in this valley, where five large haciendas were summarily handed over to their indentured labourers. They were one of the few communities well organized enough to make a go of it. Velasco's left-wing military coup was certainly intended to curb oligarchical abuses, and, as in this valley, had limited successes, but the agricultural land of the high plains and valleys has never really recovered, and the massive migration of people to the shanty towns of Lima, on the coastal desert plain, is still a desperate one-way flow.

On Independence Day, July 28th, schoolchildren parade on the village football pitch. Their grave sense of formality represents an idea, the future of their country, its glorious past, anything but themselves. The melon helmets and stick guns are as ridiculous as the goose-stepping fascist style of marching practised throughout the country by students and soldiers alike. How was it adopted and by whom? The comedy of first sight is soon silenced by the utter seriousness of it.

Five styles of masonry, all Inca, showing regional differences and perhaps from varied eras too. Where walls are extremely rough – odd stones and clay thrown together with no obvious skill in a style known as *pirca* – the walls would very possibly have been plastered and even painted with geometric patterns. This is even more likely when found alongside otherwise superlative stonework, for instance Huchuy Qosqo, the small ruins above Calca.

The retaining walls of the Temple Platform of Tarahuasi at Limatambo (top left) include flower shapes.

Qillarumi, meaning Stone Moon, has several large carved sacred rocks. Under a vast boulder, this hand-cut accentuation of a natural cave is typically abstract (bottom left).

The fine masonry of Chinchero extends to the vast terraces on which the old temples stand (far right, top).

Another view of the Tarahuasi Temple Platform, before the lichen was removed in the mid-1990s (far right, bottom).

A detail of the Temple of Viracocha, at Raqchi, to the south of Cuzco (right). It is the only known temple dedicated to the Creator-God of the Incas, and also the only example of stone pillared roof supports. The enormous scale of it alone warrants a visit.

The Yawar Fiesta, or Festival of Blood, takes place on Independence Day in the remote Apurimac town of Cotabambas. Symbolic of the continuing struggle between the Spanish and Andean cultures, the most sacred ethereal bird is connected to the furious brute strength of the foreign beast.

A week before, a mule is killed and its body placed at the bottom of a valley, over the covered pit of the condor trappers. When the gigantic scavenger comes to eat, its legs are grabbed from underneath.

Other men come running from hides nearby, yelling and waving blankets to confuse the bird, which cannot take off from the low ground without a very long run-up.

Given food and water, the condor, in this case an immature male, is well looked after in a manner befitting a sacred animal. Should any harm come to it, the omen would be dreadful. Before the fight, the condor is given *chicha* beer, both to calm it and to let it enter into the spirit of revelry. It is then carried by its wingtips

around the dry grass of the dilapidated town square before being tied with leather thongs which are sewn into the hide of the bull.

The event lasts approximately a quarter of an hour, with local men taunting the bull with capes and flags as it bucks and runs around the square. The condor flaps its enormous wings to stay balanced, and pecks at the bull's neck if the cord around its beak comes off.

Soon the bull is caught by men holding its horns and tail, and with great relief

they remove the flustered but undamaged bird. With great ceremony, it is given more beer, and townspeople file by to pay respect and have a closer look. The release of the condor is emotionally charged; it is their symbol and messenger, carrying their hopes and aspirations up to the Apus. In that moment, their next year's destiny, good or bad, takes to the sky, beyond their control again.

146

Paucartambo, a small colonial town, lies midway between the snow peaks and the jungle. In mid-July, its quiet cobbled streets are taken over by throngs of revellers during the four-day festival of the Virgin of Carmen. Troupes with elaborate costumes, masks and long-standing ritual dances, some religious others satirical, take over the town in an orgy of music and colour.

The Saqra (top right) are devils, with animal masks and bristly wigs. Here they perform their ritual dance to a band of pipes, harp and drums. (Each troupe has its own musicians and specific repeated tune.) At other times they patrol the tiled roofs and hang from the balconies around the town. The Chunchos with magnificent headdress and palm spears represent the jungle tribes never conquered by Inca or Spaniard. They form the Virgin's personal bodyguard, seen kneeling before her (left), and at the graveside of former members (centre right). Their masks are wire mesh painted with noble expressions, and one catches glimpses of the eyes behind the eyes. Contradanza are more traditionally Spanish. Made up of middle-class men from respected families, they perform dances of grace and elegance. The costumes are sewn by the dancers themselves, here in the style of a self-portrait (bottom right).

The festival descends into ritual chaos, with fireworks and battles between the groups. Oranges are fired with slings, beer is shaken and sprayed over the crowd as whipcracks and bangers punctuate the crescendo of brass bands playing ever louder to drown each other out. Pandemonium reigns. Sequined Saqra devils tow go-carts with burning wheels at high speed round and round the crowded square (right), while Qapaq Colla, the tough balaclava-wearing herders of Titicaca, jump on board, lying between the flames. Chunchos and Colla sprint in and out of the bedlam, in a symbolic war that the Chunchos always win. When caught, the Collas (ancient foe of the Incas) writhe on the ground, pinned by the spear of the dancing savage. Each repeated capture weakens them, the bamboo spikes piercing eyes and mouth register the number of 'woundings'. This Colla about to receive the third will symbolically die, in spite of his crucifix held up in defence (top left). Finally the Virgin, known as the Mamacha, Great Mother (of Christ and of Earth), appears for the last time, paraded around the streets (bottom left). The Saqras cower on the rooftops, howling and covering their eyes, while the dance groups and merry crowd fall back into order; harmony is restored for the coming year and all is well in the world.

The religious festival attracts the usual profane amusements to its fringes. Local boys poke holes to see the slick mayhem of Stallone and Van Damme for free (below), and some get their eyes poked for their trouble, while highland villagers in traditional costume swirl and dance with townspeople (left). The fusions of the festival are reflected in the temporary arcades as well, as some of the Runa girls surprise the male table-football opposition with lightning reflexes and distressingly high scores (bottom).

153

A cross leans at the edge of the highlands (below). In Peter Shaffer's play, *The Royal Hunt of the Sun*, Francisco Pizarro chides his page for his naïve chivalry faced with the bloody conquest and describes the jungle below as 'The dark we all came out of . . . Things flying, fleeing, falling dead – and their death unnoticed. Take your noble reasons there . . . wave your crosses at the wild cats. See what awe they command.' In the depths of the jungle it can seem that modern man is lost, his beliefs irrelevant. From above, all one can do is marvel, and attempt to save the diminishing Eden.

Beyond these distant outposts, the land rises once more before falling away to the forested eastern foothills and jungle beyond. At Tres Cruces (bottom), the ebb and flow of humid warmth laps at the edge of the highlands as clouds rise and fall like lungs in slumber.

From these steep heights the rivers grow in strength and momentum. The white-water rapid seen falling here in the glow of moonlight is captured by a three-minute exposure (right).

7 MACHU PICCHU

The Fabled Holy City

Equinoctial quadrant, vapour of stone.
Ultimate geometry, book of stone.
PABLO NERUDA *The Heights of Machu Picchu*

Not only has it great snow peaks looming … two miles overhead; gigantic precipices
… rising sheer for thousands of feet above the foaming, glistening, roaring rapids; it
has also, in striking contrast, orchids and tree ferns, the delectable beauty of luxurious
vegetation, and the mysterious witchery of the jungle.
HIRAM BINGHAM *Lost City of the Incas*

On an early evening, in the dry season, when the throngs have departed and shadows are stretched out on the grass, you wander around on stairs of cut stone. A morbid hush is warded off by trickling fountains and the distant footsteps and voices of the few, like you, without a train to catch. Small birds swoop in unison up over cliff-edge walls and disappear from sight. You choose a vantage point and settle. Then, in the mind's eye, hearth smoke drifts through the patterned thatch of houses, roofless now. Maize and beans are tipped out of bundles as groups of labourers return their tools, briefly silhouetted in doorways flame-lit from within. Perhaps on an altar surface, pale coca leaves twitch in the humid breeze, *chicha* froth rests on the lip of a painted bowl, and llama blood lies darkening. And someone stands watching, like you, attention focused on certain peaks and specific shadows cast across shapes in the rock.

Too few people get the chance to imagine it like this, to linger and stare. I can't help feeling sorry that the crowds are usually half their own view. Perhaps, though, that is all some want: a backdrop for portraits of themselves. And Machu Picchu has had its time alone; forgotten and smothered in 400 years of solitude.

In 1909, on a visit to Choquequirao ruins, Hiram Bingham became fascinated with the idea of Vilcabamba, the legendary lost capital city of the rebel state of the last Incas. Two years later he returned to find it. He was aware of an 1875 account by the Frenchman Charles Wiener, who had been told while in Ollantaytambo of a ruined town called 'Matcho-Picchu' to the east. It is unlikely that he had seen an 1865 map by the great Peruvian explorer Antonio Raimondi, though, on which Machu Picchu is boldly marked. Though correct about its location, neither Wiener nor Raimondi had reached it.

Following a new trail down the Urubamba gorge, Bingham was told that some ruins lay on the high ridge across the river from their camp. The informant, a local farmer named Melchor Arteaga, agreed to guide him there next day. On the morning of July 24th, 1911, Bingham's colleagues from Yale decided that the sheer 2,300-foot (700m) climb through dense and humid forest was not for them. In his 1948 recollection, *Lost City of the Incas*, Bingham quotes the naturalist as saying there were 'more butterflies near the river' while the surgeon decided he had to wash and mend his clothes.

Bingham, Arteaga and an army sergeant arrived at the ruins to find several terraces and buildings had been cleared for crops by the Alvarez family. In the Temple of the Three Windows three names were chalked on the wall, including that of Agustín Lizárraga, another local farmer from below. Bingham named him in his diary as 'discoverer of Machu Picchu'. For five hours he photographed, wrote notes and drew a sketch map. Though impressed by the masonry, he felt sure this was not Vilcabamba, as the ridge could by no means be confused with the 'wide plain' described in Spanish chronicles (opinions he later retracted after the sensational *National Geographic* article of 1913). So little impressed was he at the time that he did not return for another year, but continued on to discover Vitcos and Espíritu Pampa, and make the first ascent of Coropuna.

In 1915, and world renowned, he returned again, and discovered important ruins along an imperial road, now known as the Inca Trail. These showed that Machu Picchu was the centre of a whole region and not built in isolation. All else was speculation, including the names of buildings and sectors used to this day. Machu Picchu means Old Peak. It is unlikely that this was the town's original name. The findings of osteologist Dr George Eaton that 75 per cent of the skeletons found were female, gave rise to the myth of the Virgins of the Sun. More technological studies of the bones at Yale in the 1980s revealed a roughly equal gender split.

The forests grew back and the photographic maestro Martín Chambi took a series of fabulously overgrown views in 1925. Then, as part of the fourth centenary of the conquest in 1934, Dr Luis E. Valcárcel, a Cuzqueño archaeologist, organized the complete clearing of the vegetation. It has remained neat and tidy ever since. Bingham returned only once, in 1948, to open the road named in his honour.

In recent years, extensive surveys have been conducted by Wright Water Engineers in conjunction with Alfredo Valencia of the National Institute of Culture (INC). Their findings concur with the earlier studies of numerous archaeologists including the Cuzqueños Valcárcel and Chávez Ballón. There had been no previous settlement on the site nor had the Spaniards ever found it; some constructions were unfinished; and spacemen had not been involved. Most importantly, Kenneth Wright proved that the city was built to a definite master plan: the complicated drainage systems and spring-fed channels were intrinsic, proving that they were neither left to chance nor adapted later.

In *Machu Picchu: The Sacred Centre*, Johan Reinhard explains both the sacred geography of the area, and the extreme sanctity of its exact position on the ridge between powerful Apus (mountain gods). Standing between Cuzco and the tropical forests that provided so many luxuries, the location also made sense in strategic, political and economic terms.

The mystery surrounding its creation may finally be clearing. A document of 1568, found recently by the eminent Inca archaeologist John Rowe, refers to the estate at 'Picho', north of Cuzco, as belonging to the *Panaca* (family descendants) of the Inca Pachacuteq. It would be apt that he, the greatest Inca, credited with organizing and expanding the empire, should have had Machu Picchu constructed as his country estate, a sacred retreat from Cuzco as was the custom. It also fits with the style of architecture around 1440. Its desertion, however, remains unsolved. Dr Victor Anglés, a Cuzco historian, points out that it could not have been hidden from the Spanish and was therefore forgotten *before* the conquest.

It was customary for successive rulers to build their own new palaces, as the dead and mummified Incas family (*Panaca*) continued to look after former estates on their behalf. Whoever built Machu Picchu (Pachacuteq died in 1471), his heir Topa Inca or subsequent successors may well have preferred sites in the sunnier and less remote Sacred Valley. The torching of the city as reprisal or as a buffer zone is a possibility. The escalating costs and manpower of wars may have necessitated the withdrawal of its inhabitants, or an epidemic could have swept the province.

After a thorough evacuation that left no valuable items, there was no reason for people to go back. In a strictly controlled culture with neither written language nor freedom of movement, collective amnesia may have been quick to follow. Whatever the reasons for its abandonment, it lay shrouded in cloud forest for nearly 400 years. Opportunistic locals later encroached on its vast terraces, but no one appreciated its significance until, for one silver dollar, Melchor Arteaga brought Bingham up, and with him the continuing attention of the outside world.

Huiña Huayna (Forever Young) is the last major ruin along the Inca Trail, before one reaches Inti Punku, the so-called Sun Gate, from where one first looks down on to Machu Picchu. It lies down a dog-leg trail, which is why it wasn't found until 1941 by Paul Fejos, 26 years after the discovery of the other Inca Trail ruins. The name comes from the Epidendrum genus of orchid that flowers all year. There is also a legend that while you are standing in the circular-fronted building at the top of the terraces, you will not age a minute.

The impenetrable vegetation and sheer cliffs on which Huiña Huayna stands (far right) demonstrate clearly how these ruins remained hidden for so long, indeed how treasure hunters and explorers are seduced into the continued search for other lost ruins today. The heat, rain and insects are left to your imagination.

At the end of ten of these 6-foot (1.8m) terraces (left) stand baths, each feeding into the next, like those at Phuyupatamarca (Town in the Clouds), the previous ruin on the trail. Water was worshipped as an element, but was also used in ritual cleansing, especially (it is thought) before entering a sacred centre such as Machu Picchu.

This view directly east (above) shows the Urubamba, which is a continuation of the Vilcanota or Sacred River (confusingly, rivers change their names according to which stretch one is on). The mountain on the left horizon is Huacay Huilca (God Who Cries) also known as Veronica; thus, the ruin is linked to both these powerful deities.

The first view of Machu Picchu after the arduous Inca Trail is seen from Inti Punku, the Sun Gate (left). Huayna Picchu (Young Peak), the iconic sugar-loaf mountain, is off to the right.

A view down the slightly overgrown Machu Picchu mountain trail, a little-used but highly rewarding two-hour climb (top right). Beautifully carved stone steps and abundant wildlife enhance the incredible views.

A defensive Inca drawbridge leading away down into the valley on the far side of the city (bottom right). The vegetation below is deceptive, the cliffs are near vertical for another few hundred feet. A new Inca trail down to the river was discovered on the back of Huayna Picchu in the forest fires of 1997.

The classic postcard view of the citadel (right). The spot from which it is taken is a huge block where the Inca Trail arrives, just above the principal entrance doorway at the top of the steps in the left foreground. Large piles of exhausted trekkers collapse here, wait for the clouds to part, and have their picture taken. It is the most visited site in South America, yet still receives a tiny fraction of the numbers registered at other World Heritage sites around the globe. Strict controls are in place to ensure it remains unspoilt.

The shape of Huayna Picchu has been altered by the quarrying of rock and the construction of terraces and buildings (left). From its tip, the peak of Salcantay is visible behind Machu Picchu mountain. The changing seasons and light effects ensure that no two visits are the same.

The Intihuatana, or Hitching Post of the Sun, is the best known of Machu Picchu's many sacred carved rocks and shrines (right). Designed to hold the sun momentarily during the equinoctial moment at which the least shadow is cast by the pillar, other similar hitching posts and their functions were described by the traveller and artist Squier in the 1870s. At temples near Quito, in modern Ecuador, it was noted that the sun sat perfectly on the pillars with no shadow whatsoever, a sign of more potent sanctity. Indeed, had Atahualpa defeated the Spanish he may have decided to rule Tahuantinsuyo from Quito, the northern capital his father bequeathed him, instead of Cuzco. The shape of this Intihuatana has also been interpreted as a three-dimensional representation of Huayna Picchu, bringing that promontory's power within the temple walls.

The Intihuatana and platform shrouded in mist (above). Its position within the citadel is of paramount importance, due to complicated celestial alignments. Viewed from the sculpted shrine, the sun rises behind the powerful Apu Huacay Huilca (Veronica) on the equinox, and sets behind San Miguel, the highest point on the western horizon (Johan Reinhard located an Inca platform on this peak in the 1990s). Also from this point, on the auspicious winter solstice, the sun sets beyond Pumasillo, the most powerful mountain to the west.

The view southeast from the platform of the Intihuatana (top left). The tall peak is Machu Picchu mountain, behind which, out of sight, stands Salcantay, the most powerful local Apu. In the dip in the horizon far left, stands Inti Punku, the Sun Gate, through which the Inca Trail passes and from where the citadel was first seen by pilgrims from Cuzco.

The view from the top of Machu Picchu mountain, 1,640 feet (500m) above the main ruins (bottom left). The two sacred plazas of the Intihuatana and the Temple of the Three Windows stand light-coloured, high to the left of the main plaza. They were covered in sand in Inca times, though whether this came from the coast, as was the case in some other sacred spaces, is unknown as it has long since been dispersed by the afternoon winds.

The principal entrance to Machu Picchu, classically trapezoid, with Huayna Picchu beyond (right). The latter stands some 679 feet (207m) above the main ruins.

Buildings of the lower district, with the cliffs of Huayna Picchu beyond (far right). Strewn with epiphytes (air plants) that absorb moisture from the clouds, this view conveys something of the vertiginous terrain on all sides. From here the inaccessibility of the site is most obvious.

Putu Cusi is directly in front of the ridge on which the ruins stand (right). Beyond it, further east, the Apu Huacay Huilca peers over another high ridge where the Sun Gate is silhouetted on the horizon. There is a path up Putu Cusi, but it includes 90-foot (27m) sections of nearly vertical sawn-log ladders; with no safety rope it is quite terrifying. A plan to string a cable-car via Putu Cusi to the ruins was ill-considered and thankfully overruled by UNESCO.

The Vilcanota/Urubamba river cascades far below Machu Picchu on three sides (left). The Sacred River was believed to join up with the Milky Way at each end, beyond the horizon, explaining the reappearance of stars each day. On moonlit nights, shining silver in the dark chasm with its distant roar, the river still has the power to enchant.

Gould's Inca hummingbird (*Coeligena inca*) is so named because of its golden necklace (above). Endemic to the eastern Peruvian highland forest, it is regularly seen between the lower Inca Trail and Huiña Huayna. Gould was a nineteenth-century British ornithologist and painter whose book on hummingbirds was the definitive work for many years, and several species bear his name.

Down a precarious and exhausting trail, behind Huayna Picchu, is the cave shrine known as the Temple of the Moon (right). Some archaeo-astronomers believe it would be better known as the Temple of Pacha Mama (Mother Earth) as it is connected with her and the peak and ruins of Mandor opposite. After the fires of 1997, the trail was found to continue down to the river, passing two carved stone holes aligned with the peak of Yanantin, another possible deity connected with the cave shrine.

The interior floor of the Temple of the Sun is the top of the boulder on which it stands (top left). It has been carefully carved to capture the shape of the first rays of the sun on the June winter solstice as they pass through the trapezoidal window. The niches would have held icons, offerings and possibly llama-fat lamps.

The tiny grotto (bottom left) dubbed the Royal Mausoleum by Hiram Bingham lies between dramatically carved bedrock and the huge boulder on which stand the curved wall and carved altar of the Temple of the Sun. The position, seclusion and wonderfully intricate masonry all indicate a room of enormous spiritual importance, and the large trapezoidal niches within may well have housed royal mummies.

The Hiram Bingham Highway (left) winds nearly 7 miles (11km) up from the river to the hotel and restaurant complex. Built in 1948, it was inaugurated by Bingham himself on his first return since 1915. Here it is lit by the last workers' bus descending, in an exposure lasting a quarter of an hour. In the daytime, *chasquis* (runners) race the bus to each bend downhill, by means of shortcuts, to scream goodbye in a variety of languages. They always arrive at the bridge before the bus, clambering aboard panting for tips.

Built in a great hurry with no particular plan apart from absorbing tourist dollars, Aguas Calientes, below Machu Picchu, competes for the title of ugliest town in Peru with Juliaca, near Titicaca. It used to have a certain Wild West frontier charm, but a lavish mixture of concrete and corruption have put paid to that. The original hot baths were wiped out in a landslide by a mountain spirit offended by the sheer ghastliness of it all. Moonlight and some distance were the only way to portray it in this book (right).

8

THE CLOUD FOREST

Land of Lost Cities

Nothing gives a better idea of the density of the jungle than the fact that the savages themselves had often been within five feet of these fine walls without being aware of their existence.

HIRAM BINGHAM *Lost City of the Incas*

Blistering barnacles! Is there no end to this mountainous menagerie?

CAPTAIN HADDOCK IN *Prisoners of the Sun*

Bingham wrote the words above without ever realizing their irony. He describes standing within the 'fine walls' at Espíritu Pampa, but was unaware of their significance. They turned out to be Vilcabamba the Old, final refuge of the Incas; the place he had sought above all others. It was to be another fifty years before this was known for certain and, sadly, he was in Arlington cemetery by then.

Hung with a thick blanket of moss, the Cloud Forest is known by locals as La Ceja de la Selva, the Eyebrow of the Jungle. The fascination it inspires lies tangled in the romantic notion of things ancient and forgotten: lost ruins and undiscovered species hidden in its depths. The reality is harsh: rainfall exceeds 20 feet (6m) in an average year; tiny midges raise itching welts, their local names, *Manta Blanca* ('white blanket') and *Puma Waqachis* ('the ones who make the puma cry'), amply describing the quantity and quality of their bites; and knee-jolting trails go down 6,500 feet (2,000m) into gorges only to come up again instantly in spiteful disregard of Newton's laws. Not for nothing have ruins stayed lost for half a millennium and species survived unnamed.

There are particular types of people attracted to this habitat, obsessive people, often experts in their chosen

fields who are bored by beach holidays but are happy to sit in the cloud forest clearings, rubbing badly bitten shoulders with equally curious colleagues. Herpetologists (who chase deadly snakes), entomologists (creating names like 'Pleasing fungus beetle'), ornithologists (recording bird-calls on their Walkmans), lepidopterists (staring patiently at chrysalises), mycologists (with an unsavoury attraction to fungus) and explorers who do a lot more looking than finding, only to be rebuked for their efforts by archaeologists, the only ones sensible enough to be waiting comfortably in Cuzco. And all the while, the friendly man whose plot in which they camp would happily chop down the entire hillside and grow hamburgers on it.

Technically, at this tropical latitude, cloud forest covers the land from 3,000 to 11,500 feet (1,000–3,500m). This range of height is mirrored by the temperatures. Bingham remarked that the climates of Vitcos and Espíritu Pampa, only two days' journey apart by mule, were as alike as Scotland and Egypt. The extraordinary variety is also apparent in the wildlife, especially in the number of bird species. Ornithologists striding down the rough roads of Abra Málaga or Manu can witness the dramatic spectacle of mixed feeding flocks. Brightly coloured tanagers, brush finches, flycatchers, tree creepers and ovenbirds flitting in and out of the foliage above them in a fine example of evolutionary cohesion. It is likely that the hardcore birders will ignore these vulgar displays of 'trash' birds. They will be more attentive to the sounds of unseen dull brown species hidden in thick undergrowth with names like 'elusive ant-pitta' and 'slaty gnateater'.

The legends of Paititi and El Dorado, forbidden cities and priceless loot guarded by Amazonian tribes, began during the conquest and have not abated since. They have drawn all kinds of men, from the eccentric Colonel Fawcett, who famously disappeared in 1925 while searching, to the insanely homicidal conquistador, Lope de Aguirre. Sir Walter Raleigh was another to fall under the spell of legendary hidden Inca treasure. He had captured a homeward-bound Spanish ship carrying Pedro Sarmiento de Gamboa. Sarmiento was one of the leaders of the final expedition into Vilcabamba that had captured Tupac Amaru, the last Inca. He related stories about a younger brother of the Inca Atahualpa, fleeing north to lands laden with gold. Europe was alive with the story of Atahualpa's famous ransom, a room that had been filled with gold in the course of seven months. Raleigh persuaded Elizabeth I that he should seek such treasures and his expedition led to his founding of British Guiana, the only English-speaking country on the continent, now known as Guyana.

In the twentieth century, Bingham, Savoy, Morrison, Hemming and Lee all took part in expeditions around the Vilcabamba region, their interests more academic, but with the same fortitude as those who went before them, most notably the Peruvian explorer Antonio Raimondi whose maps of 1865 are a marvel. Less illustriously, in the 1980s, a group of Cuzco-based guides formed an exploratory club to follow up the sort of tales heard around campfires late at night: rumours of new ruins from the cook's distant cousins, friends of the horse's mouth. The Cross-Keys Ramblers, as we were known, never found Paititi – indeed, we doubted its physical existence – but to search was the stuff of childhood dreams. Small forts, centuries buried, and short stretches of Inca roads *were* found, and that was quite enough. It is hard to describe the thrill of seeing a shadowy outline in the forest gloom. The first sight of regular lines of masonry among deep moss and undergrowth is electrifying. Weeks of blood, sweat and tearful tantrums are justified by a fallen-down, historically insignificant building, smaller than a bus shelter.

For those interested in a vigorous jaunt to somewhere less crowded than Machu Picchu, Choquequirao ('Golden Cradle') is a magnificent destination. Comparable to Machu Picchu, though without the fine masonry, it has always been remote. The vistas are breathtaking and a close-up view of a soaring condor is almost guaranteed. Visits used to include a terrifying ride on an *oroya* (hanging basket) over the thunderous rapids of the Apurimac. Recently a wide trail has been laid down to the river and a concrete bridge (painted the usual vile orange) spans the rapids. The choice of visiting the ruins is hence available to the merely athletic rather than solely to the adventurous. However, all is not lost; the twelve-day trek from Vitcos on the other side is still a splendidly difficult way of getting there.

The cloud forest is a demanding domain, giving up its secrets reluctantly. For any sense of achievement, one must enjoy it for itself, like fly fishing: for its orchids, hummingbirds, swirling mist-wrapped mossy trees and endless tumbling streams.

The brave, persistent and lucky Bingham hit the biggest jackpot of all, and yet even that was a failure of sorts. Searching for forgotten Vilcabamba he found unknown Machu Picchu. Finding the real Vilcabamba, now known as Espíritu Pampa, he failed to recognize it and named Machu Picchu as the site of Vilcabamba instead. The cloud forest is like that. It will let a man discover his cake, have it and eat it and then tell him it was not a cake but a rare spongy fruit, over whose discovery two Frenchmen and an Argentinian are already fighting. There must be a lesson there somewhere. But as someone who, at the time of writing, is signed up for two expeditions to photograph a newly discovered bird, and to search for a lost city referred to in a dusty book, I am quite sure I haven't learnt it yet.

In his book *Forgotten Vilcabamba*, Vincent Lee describes how your glee diminishes as a growing list of people who have already visited, photographed and mapped out your 'new' lost city make themselves known to you. Perhaps Arlington cemetery was sanctuary for Hiram Bingham. Eight years after his death, Gene Savoy hacked his way into Espíritu Pampa and the rest is archaeology.

After the steep descent from the snowy pass of Choquetacarpo, you camp in fading light below an enchanted landscape of gigantic granite spires (top left). The next day, they watch over your transition from highlands to lowlands until, as the tree line swallows you up, they are lost to view.

A mule train appears ant-like on the cliff trails of the Apurimac canyon, ascending 6,500 feet (2,000m) to Cachora (bottom left). The *oroya* (hanging basket) used to transport people and drag horses and mules across the ferocious rapids has recently been replaced by a bridge.

On the ruined site of the Sun Temple of Chuquipalta stands Yurac Rumi or White Stone (now black with lichen), an enormous carved boulder over 65 feet (20m) wide (right). Standing below the ruined palace of Vitcos, it was the most holy of Vilcabamba temples and was also known as *Ñusta hispanan*, Where the Princess Pee'd (a name applied to various shrines placed at stream sources). A large pool once lay at its base, creating a perfect reflection. All that remains of its sacred waters are a bog and several canalized fountains beyond. Under the light of the full moon, its considerable atmosphere still takes a firm grip on you.

An *arriero* checks the overnight success of his fishing lines as dawn breaks over Waswacocha, Lake of the Ibis (left). The ibis croak and flutter away from the shore as he approaches, landing lazily only a few feet further off. It is impossible to describe the wonder of that sight on our only rest day in a two-week trek. By evening the elation was clear, the *arrieros* and cooks grinning from ear to ear at their failure to catch a fish all day, and the boisterous guzzling of surprise helpings of Easter Sunday chocolate.

A hole in the roof illuminates this stable scene (below). The moment was short-lived, as the light-filtering cloud passed clear of the harsh sun and the horse returned to chewing the side of his carved trunk trough. Both of these photographs were initiated by the excited cries of my then assistant, Quino, who would always begin, 'Far be it from me to tell you how to do your job, but . . .'

As your eye comes down from the vast landscapes to check where you might tread next, the flora and fauna of the damp terrain are revealed in distinct contrast to the barren uniformity of the highlands. Tropical abundance begins in earnest, from moss-swathed trees to epiphytes, iridescent hummingbirds, butterflies and frogs. A beetle on old man's beard (far left, top), an Andean five-bar gate post (far left, bottom), ground plants above the tree line (left), and epiphytes in the first level of forest (above), give an idea of the brilliantly coloured textures on show.

The masked trogon (*Trogon personatus*) is highly territorial, and a repeated low whistle easily calls in the male. A cousin of the quetzal, also found in this habitat, they constitute a prized sighting for any normal person but are considered 'trash birds' by accomplished ornithologists. This specimen (left) is perched in the arid forest surrounding the Inca terraces of Pincha Uñuyoc (the name refers to the spring and canalized baths there).

A male cock-of-the-rock (*Rupicola peruviana*), Peru's national bird (above). The males gather in the morning and afternoon around a specific tree to sing and dance for the drab females; this is known as a leck. The surrounding branches twitch and bounce with their ungainly bobbing up and down, and there are occasional flashes of orange as the males compete for position. Their absurd squawks are in reverse proportion to their beauty, as with so many attractive birds. The most melodious calls emerge from LBJs (little brown jobs) such as the musician wren.

Thick forest (left) turns into open ground and well-preserved Inca roads (bottom right) lead one up and up through horizontal rain and steep zigzag trails. Long waterfalls collide with cliffs, and sweat pours down one's back. When one finally staggers into the beautifully preserved ruin of Incahuasi, near Punkuyoc, a notable feature is the reflected tip of a giant rock tower in the pool below (top right). This singular aspect is all the more enigmatic for being visible only from the principal doorway. Very few people have ever been there and the clouds that rush up and obliterate all views add to the atmosphere. What lies atop the tower, or at its foot? Buried treasure? X marks the spot! But when will one ever return?

An overview of the plaza and main buildings of Choquequirao (left). Like Machu Picchu, 30 miles (50km) or so away to the northeast over the Cordillera Vilcabamba, it straddles a natural spur towards the end of a descending ridge. Overlooked for many years due to its apparently crude masonry, its size and position suggest it was a centre of some importance. Vincent Lee, who discovered and documented a large previously unknown group of buildings here in the 1990s, goes so far as to suggest it may have been built for Topa Inca, son of Pachacuteq, and great consolidator of his father's conquests. The snow peaks of the Vilcabamba range to the left include the powerful Apu Pumasillo (Puma's Claw).

Sunset casts the glow across the plaza that gives the ruin its name (below, top left). The area of flat ground is put to splendid use by the cooks and *arrieros* as a championship football pitch. After 11 days of hard trekking, they reveal the contents of their tiny backpacks: full kit, including studded boots and numbered shirts. To see them all bent double, for 15 minutes at a time, bellowing instructions to an unfortunate sent to retrieve the ball from the forested ravine is a rare treat.

The Southern Cross descends behind a moonlit wall, the trapezoidal niche and window classically Inca (below, top right). The crude masonry has been explained by US geologist and explorer Gary Ziegler as

a result of the metamorphic rock that cannot be hewn like the interlocking granite of other sites. (Kuelap and K'anamarca are similarly constructed for the same reason.) The amount of cement used and white-painted reconstruction guides are the fault of Copesco, a government development agency.

The view from the main plaza shows the raging waters of the Apurimac (God Who Speaks) some 6,000 feet (1,800m) below (below, bottom right). Like Machu Picchu, the proximity of the Sacred River and Apus to the west would have influenced the choice of Choquequirao's location.

Standing above a beautifully intact 10-foot (3m) wide Inca road, these terraces (below, bottom left) are 1,150 feet (350m) long and over 20 feet (6m) high. Recently, over 120 of them have been discovered on the forested slopes around the ridge spur. This rivals the famous spectacle of Pisaq, and, with a new easier two-day trail, Choquequirao is expected to attract many visitors who have already seen Machu Picchu.

187

A fortunate piece of behavioural ecology is that of all the ridges in the canyon, the local population of condors favour this one; they rise each afternoon from cruising the depths below. More than a dozen will pass only feet above one's head in the course of an afternoon spent exploring the site (far left, top).

A view of the Río Blanco valley (top left) exemplifies the precipitous terrain surrounding the ruins. The shock of the knee-straining descent of 8,500 feet (2,600m) through dusty arid woodland and cactus is softened only by the even more appalling climb up the other side. Finally

reaching the ridge to the side of the ruins, one is back in the mossy habitat of true cloud forest. It is often the case here that the shaded side of a ridge will have far more lush vegetation due to the moisture conserved.

Pieces of ceramic found at the site include this condor's head from the coast (bottom left) and a head of maize. The rather crude objects made at Choquequirao, like the *chicha* jar fragment representing a llama, at centre, display the same silver flecks as the ground below. The flecks are muscovite mica, and ceramics displaying this effect are known as Vilcabamba style. There is

silver nearby that was mined by the Incas and Spaniards alike, but mica is fool's silver.

A small pair of buildings stand either side of a courtyard, well away from the rest of the ruins (far left, below). The clear view both ways down the sacred canyon suggests a spiritual use. It may have been a retreat for the Inca or high priest. Then again, it may simply have served as a watch tower. With Inca archaeology there is much guesswork and little proof.

The archetypal view of a lost city before the indiscriminate clearing and ghastly

reconstructions begin (below). A vast hall with 14 niches along its supporting wall, this was first surveyed and documented in 1996 by Vincent Lee, the North American architect-explorer. Lee's stunningly detailed plans of the major ruins of the region appear in his book, *Forgotten Vilcabamba*.

Falsely known as Andean pine, because of its needles, the species is actually a *Podocarpus glomeratus*. This giant (left) in the National Park of Ampay, above the city of Abancay, is at least 500 years old, and stood as a young sapling when Pizarro and his men rode fighting through the valley below. Known locally as El Progenitor, Father of the Forest, there are approximately 50 trees of a similar age above the first lake. Moss, lichen and clouds smother everything in Ampay, giving it an other-worldly quality. The strange mix of trees and plants is to be found only in the microclimate at the top end of this valley, hence the designation and protection of its park status.

Passing the still waters of the lower lake in thick, drizzling rain, a shepherd boy (right) gathers his family's sheep and moves them from the forest to a safer pasture. A rusty bunch of old tin cans hang from the lead sheep's neck; the others follow the sound, which is supposed to keep pumas at bay.

Cloud forest at mid-afternoon. One feels almost under water when the thickest fog rolls up from the jungles below. It is easy to become disorientated, and a compass and whistle are mandatory. Even thin branches appear four times their size, swollen with soaking spongy moss. Leaning against a tree, one is instantly wet through from shoulder to ankle. The terrain is steep, with precipices hidden by the vegetation and clouds. The wonder isn't that so many lost ruins abound here, but why people put up with these conditions to find them. The swollen caterpillars, fungi and lichen are in their element.

Espíritu Pampa, site of Vilcabamba the Old, was the last refuge of the Incas and the legendary capital of the rebel state of Vilcabamba. Lost for centuries and overlooked by Hiram Bingham in 1911, who thought the little he saw of it too crude to be an imperial city, it was finally cleared in 1964–5 by Gene Savoy, the flamboyant US explorer. The site and layout matched physical descriptions taken from contemporary Spanish chronicles, but the conclusive pieces of evidence were broken clay roof tiles littering the forest floor and a buried layer of ash found by Howell and Morrison's expedition of 1966. John Hemming put the last piece of the puzzle in place when reading a lost part of a chronicle by the priest Martín de Murúa, which had been rediscovered in 1945 by the 7th Duke of Wellington among papers the 1st Duke had captured from Napoleon. In it, Hemming noted a specific passage describing Vilcabamba as having had tiled roofs (a Spanish innovation as the Incas used thatch) and that the city had finally been torched by the fleeing Incas themselves. With the legwork and thorough fieldnotes of the three expeditions and Murúa's text, Hemming's patient research had found the definitive proof. Largely forgotten again, due to its remote location and terrorist activity in the region, the vegetation grew back until Vincent Lee's thorough and excellent surveys of the 1990s. The forest continues to reclaim the area at present, which seems fitting for a lost city. Here one sees the rustic masonry smothered by trees (left) and the famously conclusive roof tiles, strewn across the ground, and the buttress roots of a jungle giant (below).

At Vista Alegre on the trail from Huancacalle, a local woman contemplates a trekking group struggling down the muddy trail (below). The prevailing attitude to tourists returning to the region after a 10-year enforced absence (terrorism was rife here in the mid-1980s) is a typically timid and gravely well-mannered welcome. (Though it is hard not to believe that they generally consider one at worst a grave robber and at best simply mad.)

End-of-the-road towns are the same the world over. Meagre commerce sustains a ragtag community on a frontier between vehicle and mule tracks. The bare necessities are to be had, but no frills. Skinny dogs lie around and maybe the odd vulture. Depending on whether you are driving in or walking out, they can be your personal heaven or hell. Here at Chuanqiri (right), the wild enthusiasm for a plate of fresh chicken has developed into a strong desire to get the hell out and on back to civilization, as the rain gets heavier and the chance of a truck ever slimmer.

9 MADRE DE DIOS

The Tropical Rainforest

The land is one great wild, untidy luxuriant hothouse,
made by nature for herself.
CHARLES DARWIN *Voyage of the Beagle*

Madre de Dios in southern Peru may have the richest animal life of any
region on earth.
ADRIAN FORSYTH (AND KEN MIYATA) *Tropical Nature*

My first impression of the Amazon jungle, on a moonless night in 1985, was when something enormous bolted through the undergrowth alongside my rather flimsy and low-slung hammock . . . then . . . silence. As I lay rigid, breath held, with heart and bowels leaping around, I stared out into the pitch black and saw only darkness. 'Don't worry, it's probably just as scared of you,' came a voice from an extremely secure tent nearby.

An inspection of tracks at daybreak revealed that a tapir, browsing herbivore and South America's largest animal, had indeed been as startled as I was (after an initial burst of speed, they creep away in stealth mode); yet in spite of our intimate encounter, it was to be another two years before I actually set eyes on one.

A visit to the tropical rainforests of the Americas, unlike the Great Barrier Reef or the Serengeti Plains, is nothing like a television documentary where animals appear from every angle to copulate and eat each other. You could walk past a big cat, a few feet away in the foliage, and never know how close you came; and this is another distinctive feature of the New World tropics: the lack of dangerous predators. The voice from the tent was right when it said not to worry, but not necessarily

because the animals are scared; the reason is that their patterns of hunting and diet evolved long before man's relatively recent arrival. Unless you molest an animal or 'cross some ancient predator–prey chain', as Alex Shoumatoff puts it in *The Rivers Amazon*, you are generally safe. Having spent much time there, I can honestly say that I feel safer walking trails at night in Amazonia than in many of the world's larger cities, notwithstanding the faint unease experienced walking solo anywhere on a dark night.

The absence of easily seen wildlife can increase one's appreciation of the habitat itself, as other senses are brought into focus. It is the mysterious noises and pungent smells that strike one when entering the forest for the first time. Stepping out of harsh sunlight into the cooler gloom, one can begin to comprehend how much heat the trees absorb, a first clue as to their global worth. As your eyes adjust to the filtered-green light, you are struck by the immensity of the vegetation, from leaves to buttressed trunks. Though some biologists groan at comparisons with cathedrals, there is no doubt that one does stare up into a vast enclosed space and wonder about God.

A visit to Madre de Dios, whether to Manu National Park or the Tambopata Candamo Reserve, will begin with a guided trip on one of the tributaries of the Amazon. This far up-river the banks are close enough on both sides to be clearly visible, unlike its mouth where it flows 100 miles (160km) wide. A guide in the forest plays much the same role as subtitles on a foreign film. The trail systems are designed to lead you through a maximum variety of habitats, and, as general tendencies are explained and emphasis is placed on specific interactions, patterns begin to emerge.

Those with childhood memories of dull lessons needn't worry; the experience of learning about a wild animal's behaviour as it stands before you is a very long way from the whiff of formaldehyde in the school laboratory.

In secondary 'disturbed' forest, often at the edge of clearings or water, the vegetation is impregnably thick. Fast-growing plants such as bamboo, balsa and the ubiquitous white trunks and open-fingered leaves of the cecropia tree rapidly fill in any gaps. In their fight for light, the cecropias favour speed over defence. To compensate, they provide shelter and high carbohydrate capsules for azteca ants which reciprocate by protecting the tree from herbivorous insects and swarming out to attack larger animals that disturb their home. The sloth is often found in cecropias too, and, moving slowly enough not to provoke the aztecas, makes a lengthy feast of the leaves. At great personal risk and expense of energy, the sloth descends to bury its dung pellets at the base of the tree, thus returning around half of the nutrients eaten and helping sustain its food source.

Each pattern of behaviour is founded on selfish ends, but the immense period of evolutionary time has bonded them in a way that appears less so. In extreme examples there are some species that are totally dependent on each other, like the leaf-cutter ant and the fungus that it grows. The ants farm the fungus on a chewed leaf mulch and the fungus feeds the ants with fruiting bodies; without each other they cannot exist.

In swamp forest, the trees are spaced apart with little lower vegetation in the brackish water. Stilt palms, both open and closed, are a common sight. Their roots, standing some 3 feet (1m) high like tens of tripod legs, sprout from the base of the trunk. As they droop down on a slow journey to the ground, others on the opposite side will often be allowed to rot away, creating the legend 'trees that walk' (an open-stilt palm may move several inches over a few years). Far more interesting to many visitors is the fact that the growing roots bear more than a passing resemblance to large if flaccid male reproductive organs. It is a challenge to stop groups tearing off a few for a snapshot, especially when you did exactly the same thing yourself (many years ago).

Climbing up steep clay banks one finally reaches the primary, high forest, known as *tierra firme*. This is the jungle as seen so often on film and television, and it fulfils most visitors' mental image of the jungle. The clay cliffs which have caused you to stand panting and sweating, reveal the first 30–40 feet (9–12m) of infertile clay lying up to nearly 2 miles (3.3km) deep; the eroded and leached remains of the massif that stood to the west before the Andes rose up. Deposited here at the end of the Cenozoic era some 2–4 million years ago, they are virtually devoid of inorganic nutrients. As you stand there surrounded by the gigantic trunks of brazil nut, strangler fig and mahogany, it doesn't seem possible that the ground beneath your feet is infertile. Scrape away the leaf litter with the toe of your boot and you will find the truth, a fine white mesh of thousands of rootlets and fungal threads, busily and invisibly breaking down and recycling the all-important minerals like potassium and phosphorus that sustain the giants above. The entire forest floor is a constant powerhouse of regeneration – each dead leaf, fallen twig, piece of dung and feather is fed back into the system by a host of fungi, beetles and termites. The pervasive smell of the forest is this rapid turnover of its own highly accelerated compost. Kick your heel in hard and you see just below the surface the same leached red clay so obvious on the bare cliffs. The nutrients do not sink in and, obviously, as we have seen on television, when the trees are cut and burnt, the rains wash away whatever nutrients are left. The unshaded clay is baked hard and the land rendered practically useless.

On the printed page it is a much repeated and therefore unmoving lecture, especially as the rainforests are as familiar to most people as the surface of the moon, seen merely through media. Human beings have made an art form of denial and, like intelligent smokers, we are all well aware of the problem. A visit to the tropical rainforest is like having a chest X-ray: suddenly the problem becomes shockingly urgent and real.

Descending from the high forest it is likely that the trail will eventually reach a lagoon, or *cocha* as they are known locally. These ox-bow lakes, former bends of the river cut off by erosion, provide some of the best opportunities to view wildlife. Egrets, herons, kingfishers and neotropical cormorants abound. Out on the water, a catamaran raft provides a better angle from which to observe the canopy and layers of the forest. A fruiting tree on the water's edge will bring many species together for an opportunistic feast and you may even see an eagle take a monkey while an entire troop dives for cover, screeching alarm and outrage as they shake the branches in defiance. Fallen trees provide limited piers on the water, where side-necked turtles stack up to sun themselves and birds keep an eye on the fish.

If very fortunate and silent, you may even see larger mammals like tapir or puma swimming, or the cruising head of a usually nocturnal 16-foot (5m) long, black caiman (South America's giant crocodilian). If you are deep inside a reserve, one of the most dramatic potential sightings is of giant river otters. Known in Spanish as *lobos del río*, or river wolves, they grow to over 6 feet (1.8m) long, often hunting in extended family groups. Their rarity is not the only obstacle to finding them; they move for several days at a time to different lakes so as to satisfy their phenomenal appetite without exhausting the supply of fish. Visits by tourists to more than one lake are often discouraged as it has been shown that the stress of frequent contact with humans may affect birthrates. With no more than 600 pairs left in the wild, this is a grave concern. (The undisturbed habitat needed to support a viable population, that is, one capable of sustaining a large gene pool, has been calculated at a million hectares. The same applies to other large predators, including jaguar, and it is ominous indeed that few parks in the world outside Manu meet this criterion.) Each of these species – side-necked turtle, black caiman and giant river otter – is categorized as highly endangered, hunted to near extinction in the 1950s. Today, national parks are their only hope of survival in the wild.

Canopy platforms and walkways some 140 feet (42m) up are another means of viewing wildlife with relative ease, and they offer a view into an ecosystem virtually unknown to scientists just thirty years ago. There are many species that live out their entire lives among the treetops; their behavioural evolution keeping them from predators or rivals that have taken up other ecological niches below them.

After several hours of walking slowly through all these habitats, the knowledge gained provides great satisfaction, and the far-flung repetition has you passing familiar things. You are aware that the explosive bursts of scampering by your feet are merely lizards (though they still make you jump), that the plant like a spiral staircase grows that way to ensure no leaf shades another from photosynthetic light (you never thought you'd pronounce photosynthesis, let alone understand it). Some of those eerie sounds actually tell you things; the staggered collisions of falling vegetation can be ignored (unless heard overhead – statistically Amazonia's most common cause of death), while continued irregular crashing signals monkeys on the move. People who at dawn expected several phobic fits an hour begin to feel at home; some would-be David Attenboroughs even correct less attentive members of the group ('Those leaf-cutter ants don't eat the leaves, they grow fungus on them. No ant, no fungus and vice versa').

I remember a group of Australians, one day into their trip, asking to go off the reserve to catch a piranha, a special birthday treat for the youngest, who was seventy-nine that day. At sunset, quietly paddling a canoe, our peace was shattered by a raucous flock of macaws, flying in pairs back to their hollow palm-trunk roosts.

'Macaws,' said one, with great authority.

'Anyone knows a macaw, mate! What type?'

'They're not a type, they're a species,' with binoculars raised. 'And they're blue and yellah.'

'They can live to over eighty and mate for life,' I added.

'No wonder they make such a bloody racket, I know how they feel!'

The relaxed laughter as we walked back to the lodge in darkness was a far cry from the hesitant questions about spiders and snakes that morning.

Madre de Dios is a haven for scientists and tourists, drawn by the world records of biodiversity. A sign at Puerto Maldonado airport proclaims: 'Welcome to the Biological Capital of the World' (though the plea not to buy pets and skins has been heavily defaced). Sadly for the original inhabitants, rubber, gold, oil and the promise of free land have brought successive invasions of outsiders, ignorant about sustainable development. It is ironic that jungle tribes are the victims of modern invasion, as the rainforests were the only region near Cuzco where the Inca empire failed in its expansion.

Those tribes that populated the area over 10,000 years ago are diverse in themselves, with more than seven known linguistic groups. Most of them are acculturated, including the largest group, the Machiguenga (Arawakan), whose trading contact with the Incas is still evident in the Quechua words in their language. The Piros (also Arawakan), who were used to enslave other tribes by Fitzcarraldo during the rubber boom, are settled in two areas, the upper Urubamba from where they came, and the upper Madre de Dios, their route home blocked by vengeful tribes still inhabiting the headwaters of the Manu river. Among these uncontacted tribes are the Amahuaca and the Mashco Piro (Harakmbet) who still live a stone-age existence, their survival ensured by a no-go area within Manu park and their notorious hostility to outsiders. The Esse Eja (Tacanan) – described in the 1920s as the 'fierce Guarayo' by the explorer Colonel Fawcett – live peacefully along the banks of the Tambopata and Heath rivers.

Some of the villages are involved in eco-tourism and research into ethno-botany, their knowledge of medicinal plants being of global significance. The defensive chemical arsenal of the trees and animals of the rainforest has contributed to over 50 per cent of our medicines, from the curare of poison arrow frogs (muscle relaxant in surgery) to the quinine under the bark of the cinchona tree (anti-malarial drugs), and it is the shaman of any village who is the 'librarian of the forest', with his extensive recognition of these plants and knowledge of their uses. As a new generation, uninterested in traditional medicine, grows up with Teletubbies and chainsaws, the plants from which their modern drugs are derived are being forgotten. Other plants disappear before they are even named, let alone studied.

As more people visit the forests of Amazonia, they take home first-hand knowledge and stories and many send friends, or return themselves. Eco-tourism is a fast-growing industry that, carefully managed, can benefit local people while preserving the habitat. It is an activity where familiarity breeds concern; if tourists both from the Amazonian countries and abroad begin to see the rainforest as an Eden, not a green hell, and if governments see the long-term commercial value in these exploits rather than the shorter-term riches of extraction, then perhaps it will exist for our grandchildren.

On a night as dark as my first I was given another fright, but this time by something a lot smaller than a tapir. Returning to camp I was horrified to find coin-sized holes in my tent: leaf-cutter ants had begun to harvest my home. I knew that if they kept going, the whole thing would be gone in under an hour. Crawling slowly inside, I sprayed repellent at the affected areas and plugged the holes with gaffer tape. While I sat in the middle of the tent and imagined dawn breaking over two naked tent poles and my swollen remains, the ants were assuming that my repellent was the 'plant' defending itself. Using alarm chemistry of their own, they gave a signal to cease work and left to find some other less hostile crop. For some time I was unaware of my triumph, sitting bolt upright every few minutes with torchbeam flying to every corner of the tent. After about twenty minutes, and no mass entry, I stuck my head outside and saw that they had gone. My relief was combined with the realization that, for a brief moment, I had ceased to be an observer and had participated in some complicated form of ecological behaviour. I had resisted the attack of several thousand highly evolved and motivated creatures, and sent them off to another piece of their territory. Once again I felt at home, the chorus of the jungle night surrounding me, and my pulse slowed as I lay back and slept the sleep of the recently uneaten.

Two views of Cocha Salvador, a large ox-bow lake deep inside Manu National Park and Biosphere Reserve (left). With a healthy population of caiman and a family of giant river otters, it is a required stop for tourists and wildlife cameramen alike. It lies two days' boat-ride up the Manu river.

The approach to Boca Manu airstrip (top right) shows clearly how the ox-bow lakes are formed, as bends in the river erode in on themselves and get cut off. The lakes or *cochas*, the Quechua term, eventually silt up and grow in; it is thought that virtually all lowland forest has at one time or another been a lake bed.

The rivers are the highways of the forest. A boat returns home, viewed from Sunset Point on the Explorer's Inn reserve on the Tambopata river (bottom right). As the river reflects almost the entire sky on this sweeping bend, a fan-like effect often occurs at sunset, with the Andes sending shadows across the evening like the Japanese rising sun motif. More than one proposal of marriage has been accepted here, and several thousand cold beers too.

A former river rapid dries out in the evening sun (below). The top and bottom of the picture are water; the major flow having moved off right to a shallower route as the water levels fall. The swirled mud dries eventually to sand, seen abutting the rocks above. At the line where mud and sand meet on the upper right, a human boot print can be seen for scale.

A portrait of a black caiman, largest of South America's crocodilians and a species hunted nearly to extinction in the 1950s. This specimen on Cocha Juárez (right) was implicated in a tourist's demise, though it is thought the man had drowned beforehand. Caiman are generally unaggressive towards humans, but swimming at night is not recommended. Another colourful chapter in this caiman's life occurred when it tried to take a young giant river otter, whose extended family swiftly retaliated by chewing off one of its front legs. It is thought to have been born in 1985, and now measures over 16 feet (5m). This picture was taken when it had four legs and no criminal record.

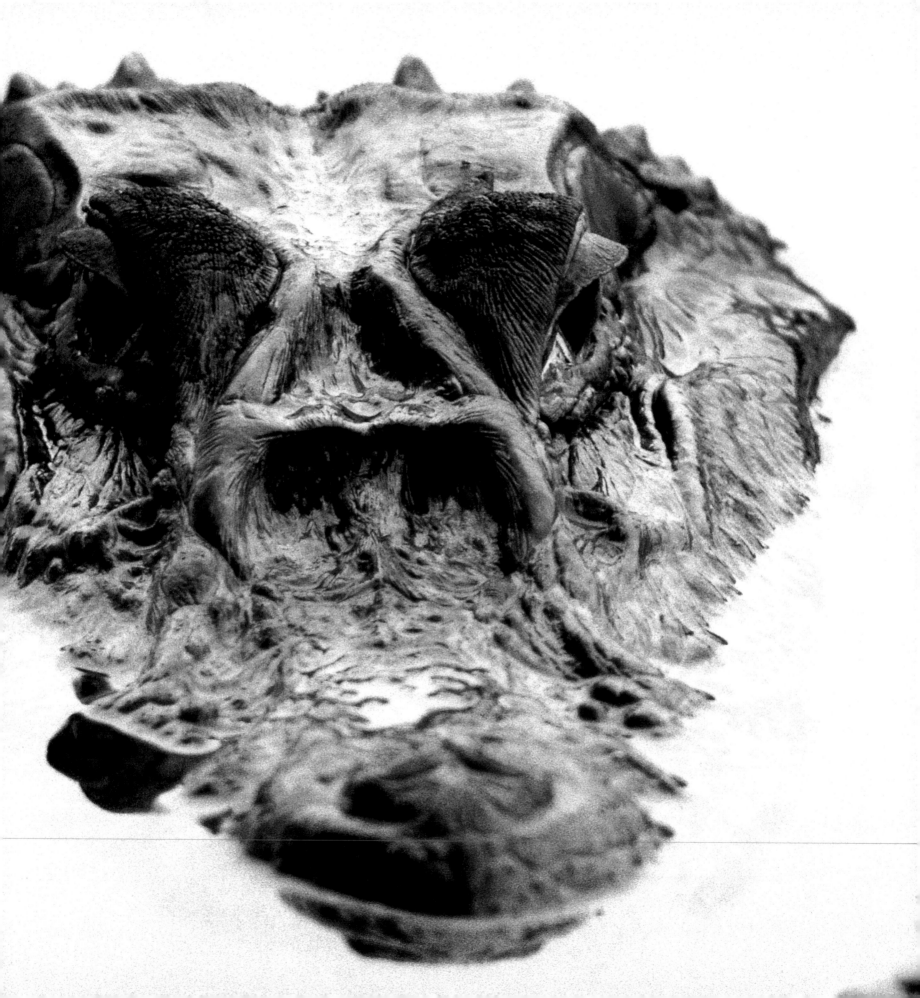

Champions in the battle for photosynthetic light: four views of some of the forest's elder statesmen.

A detail near the base of a strangler fig, *Ficus ypsilophlebia* (left). This giant begins life as a defecated seed, high in the canopy. It sends filament roots down several hundred feet that eventually swell, surround and smother the host; a murder lasting up to 200 years leaves only the fig standing. The hollow centre is all that remains of the former emergent.

The view from quarter of the way up a kapok or lupuna tree, *Ceiba pentandra* (right). The vast branches of the kapok begin to spread at over 100 feet (30m) high, and are often thicker than the trunks of their neighbours. The largest species of trees, which grow up to 80 feet (25m) higher than the surrounding canopy, are known as emergents. Buttress roots that spread thick and shallow around the base (here hosting nine eco-tourists) are a misnomer; they act more like guy ropes.

One has to walk a long way, in deep protected reserves, to find a specimen of mahogany (*Swietenia macrophylla*) as large as this one (far right, top) in the reserve surrounding Manu Wildlife Centre, just outside the park. Threatened by the voracious harvest for fine furniture, these trees will not grow in plantations, but need the protection of hundreds of other species to survive. It is rare to find any emergent growing in groups, usually they are found at least 300 feet (100m) apart.

The variety of strategies used to capture light and nutrients is vast (far right, bottom). Speed of growth, shape of leaves and symbiotic relationships built over evolutionary millennia are some of the systems used. Vines use the piggy-back method, sometimes so successfully that their weight can help pull down their host. Statistically, falling vegetation is the biggest threat to human life in the forest. When camping out, the first thing to be done is to look up and check for dead-looking branches known as widow-makers.

The fabulously camouflaged horned toad (*Ceratophrys cornuta*) is a triumph of evolution and a favourite find (above). Its other name – large-mouthed toad – is warranted. Essentially a mouth with feet, it awaits a wide-ranging menu, including katydids, frogs and even other toads.

The male rhinoceros beetle, *Megasoma elephas* (top right), uses its horns to fight others by tipping them on to their backs. Both genders are defended by a tough outer shell, covering wings that span over 6 inches (15cm); in flight they sound like a medium-sized helicopter. The sight of a large American lady careering round with a beetle diving to investigate her red shirt

or perfume is something I shall never forget. The local shaman was very impressed by the depth of her screams and the fluidity of her movements.

Having soaked up heat, this tiny lizard disappears through the hole in the leaf (far right, top). Certainly, in the shade its dark shape is better hidden.

A male lizard, *Ameiva ameiva* (centre right), pauses while following a female (her green rear legs visible behind his nose). As a means of escape, lizards run in short explosive bursts through the dry leaf litter. The sudden sound from near your feet never fails to make you jump.

Snakes are rarely encountered in the forest; speed walking is one way of catching timid snakes by surprise, though the shock felt is often mutual. Here a *Chironius exoletus* (far right, centre) freezes on a trail.

One of the hundreds of species of frog within Manu Park is the hatchet-faced tree frog, *Sphaenorhynchus lacteus* (bottom right). Archie Carr summed up their charm in *The Windward Road*: 'I like the look of frogs, and their outlook, and especially the way they get together in wet places on warm nights and sing about sex.'

Caterpillars huddled together appear as one large beast (bottom centre). Should any

predator not be fooled, their chemical arsenal is extremely potent. The black dots are small seeds dislodged in their nocturnal voyage to the canopy.

A tree boa (*Corallus enydris*) awaits small birds and rodents (far right, bottom). Though trying to look threatening, it is harmless. The deadly snake genus of the region includes the emerald tree viper (*Bothrops bilineatus*), lanceheads (*Bothrops* spp.), coral snakes (*Micrurus* spp.) and the awesome bushmaster (*Lachesis muta*) that despite its lethal venom and potential 12-foot (3.5m) length, is generally docile, even banging its tail in warning when approached by birdwatchers looking skywards.

The dim, green world of the under-canopy is relieved by shafts of light, myriad shapes and textures and bright blossoms either alive or in a thick fallen carpet on the forest floor (left). Here the acanthaceae (*Aphelandra aurantiaca*) blooms, leaves are backlit, and a squirrel monkey (*Saimiri sciureus*) peers through leaves of the Mauritius palm (*Mauritia flexulosa*), a favourite source of food for the troops of up to 100 individuals.

Coated with dawn dew, the webs of community spiders cover a Lima tree (above). Among the thousands of hard-working social spiders lives one of the tourists' favourites: the klepto-parasite spider (*Argyrodes ululans*), aka the Yuppie Spider. Within the protection of their city he builds himself a penthouse suite, and whenever something good gets trapped nearby, he will zoom out in the opposite direction and jump about like a spider possessed. The little spiders will go to investigate, then he sprints back, grabs the prey, takes it home and shuts the door. There are numerous examples of dishonesty in nature, but few quite so engaging and flamboyant.

Extremely shy and mostly nocturnal, the ocelot, *Felis pardalis* (left), is one of the forest's greatest sightings. Unlike other large felines, it maintains the delicate shape of a domestic cat though standing as tall as a German shepherd. Endangered due to the popularity of its skin in the mid-twentieth century, the ban on trading has led to a dramatic increase in its population, though farmers still shoot them on sight as they are attracted to easy prey. The illegal capture of macaws, parrots and monkeys for the pet trade is a huge problem, and this jaguar's skull found by park guards (top right) symbolizes the sickening continued market for spotted cat pelts. The surprisingly agile white caiman, *Caiman crocodilus* (bottom right), was never in the same danger as its larger black relatives who are still on the red data list of species threatened with extinction.

Butterflies lap minerals from the eyes and nostrils of side-necked turtles, *Podocnemis unifilis* (bottom left). Visible in the water behind, other turtles queue up like planes at an airport to sun themselves on the limited piers of fallen trees. Each time one plops back into the cooling water, a replacement shuffles up from behind, joining stacks sometimes 12 long.

In the same search for scarce minerals, a group of pieridine butterflies (top left) absorb minerals from the urine of capybaras, deposited on this beach half an hour before.

One of the largest varieties in the world, a Rothschild's moth, *Saturniidae Rothschildia* sp. (top right) spreads its 8-inch (20cm) wingspan as the sun sets. It is also known as the window-winged saturnian, due to the four transparent grey patches on the darker purple inner wing.

A tree frog lands briefly on an open leaf (bottom right), but before it has time to change colour takes off again to a shadier spot. I tried to catch it, but a series of rapid haphazard leaps succeeded where camouflage was too slow. The same thing happened with three different poison arrow frogs, which were so quick I failed to get a single image.

Pancho, a relatively tame blue and yellow macaw (*Ara araraura*), wonders if he could take a better picture (left). Having appeared on the cover of *National Geographic*, I half expect him to correct my focusing skills. Macaws are extremely intelligent and sociable. They mate for life and need constant attention. In captivity they are prone to pull out their feathers when bored. Having seen them wheeling through the gaps in forest trees and watched pairs pass by every sunset chattering constantly to each other, there could be no pleasure in owning a clipped captive. I once arrived at the Tambopata *colpa* (salt-lick) two days after poachers had shot several of them. It was heart-rending to watch a macaw as it wheeled round and round above us, calling out for its dead mate.

The giant tinamou (*Tinamus major*) makes its shallow nest between the buttress roots of larger trees (above). Whether the colour of the eggs deters predators is not known. Certainly, when in residence, the partridge-like bird is virtually invisible against the brown leaves and trunk. Happening upon a nest unawares on two occasions, I have learnt that they sit still before detonating past your knees at the last moment. The effect on one's heartrate is noteworthy, especially as the gigantic and deadly bushmaster viper lives in these same niches.

A common potoo, *Nyctibius griseus* (right), is a rare sight due to its tree-like plumage. Its nocturnal call, a series of five descending notes, is one of the most amusing sounds of the jungle, very much like the patronizing series of 'yeah's one gets from someone who's heard it all before. Its larger relative, the great potoo, is also famous for its call, a two-note squawk that can be heard half a mile away. I once played a tape of insects, frogs and birds through huge speakers at midnight on the roof of Christ Church, Oxford. The potoos received a terrific ovation.

Just before dawn a black vulture, *Coragyps atratus* (top left), sits in its customary tree, with 11 others above and below. The nostril for scent and claws for holding flesh still to tear are clear against first light. Though carrion eaters, they seem to have evolved a predilection for the rubbish tips outside any human dwellings; tayras, large marten-like creatures, can often be found in this same habitat.

An anhinga, *Anhinga anhinga* (bottom left), dries its wings and warms its blood after a lengthy dive. A relative of the cormorant, its habit of swimming with only its neck showing gives it the local name of snakebird. They spear fish while swimming under water, rather than using the momentum of a gannet-like dive.

Hoatzins, *Opisthocomus hoazin* (top right), are notable for a claw on the end of their wings, which they lose as adults. Whether this is an ancient feature linking them to archaeopteryx or an evolutionary coincidence (the young jump into water below nests as an escape, then use the claws to climb back up when danger is past) is the subject of some debate. Also known as stinkbirds for obvious reasons, they appear to the casual observer to be fantastically stupid.

In *A Parrot without a Name*, Don Stap describes their hapless gliding flight, 'invariably crash-landing into bushes,

where they usually knock several of their kind off balance and start a ruckus of loud disgruntled croaking.'

Dead trees on ox-bow lakes provide piers for turtles, perches for kingfishers and neotropical cormorants and a safe nest site for a red-capped cardinal, *Paroaria gularis* (bottom right). Its bright orange eye stays on us as the catamaran raft passes slowly away along the tangled shoreline in search of herons and a dancing sun bittern.

Red and green macaws (*Ara chloroptera*) wheel away from the *colpa* at some suspected danger (bottom left). When perched on the open cliffs, they are very vulnerable to birds of prey and even ocelot. The slightest noise or shadow will scare them away, from a small landslide to any large bird flying overhead. Waiting noisily in the surrounding trees (top left), they will eventually return to the clay cliffs again. Their hesitancy each day means that they always let the parrots feed first.

Mealy parrots (*Amazona farinosa*), blue-headed parrots (*Pionus menstruus*) and orange-cheeked parrots (*Pionopsitla barrabandi*) gather each dawn to consume clay on a *colpa* (top right). Aiding digestion of a caustic diet (many plants have chemical defences), many species of animal visit similar sites, including tapir and howler monkeys.

Sand-coloured nighthawks (*Chordeiles rupestris*) use a large dead tree, mid-river, safely to snooze the afternoon away (bottom right). Equally, if not better, camouflaged on beaches, they live in large colonies seeking protection in numbers as well. Their eggs are the same speckled sandy colour. As boats approach camp at the end of day, it is a great spectacle to watch massive flocks lift off from the shores and wheel alongside, grabbing the evenings insects as they go.

One of the rarest mammals on the planet, giant river otters (*Pteronura brasiliensis*) grow to over 6 feet (1.8m) long and live in family groups on large ox-bow lakes (left). Hunting in packs for seven hours in the 12-hour day, and catching 9lb (4kg) of fish, they are known as *lobos del río* (river wolves) in Spanish. Their territories often take in several lakes so as not to exhaust the food supply. Young and solitary otters are vulnerable to black caiman, but the teeth seen in the picture below can tear fist-sized bites out of the predators' soft underbellies, and when under a sustained attack, the caiman appear to try to run across the surface to escape. Jaguar and anaconda are no match for them either; man is their only real enemy. Between the Second World War and 1970 over 24,000 of their pelts were exported from Peru alone, and now no more than 600 pairs are thought to survive in the wild. Tourist visits are strictly controlled by biologist guides, as the stress caused by repeated close contact can effect birthrates. Ideally, a sufficient distance is kept so that the spluttered alarm call is avoided, but if it is heard, should be immediately acted upon by a swift withdrawal.

A family of 14 capybara (*Hydrochoerus hydrochaeris*) amble away from the sound of the approaching boat engine (right). They are the world's largest rodent, weighing up to 140lb (65kg), and their defence system of diving for long periods then reappearing some distance away is effective when faced with their main enemy, the jaguar (*Panthera onca*). A benefit of visiting this area, besides the world's highest biodiversity, is the proximity of both shores, with any animal sightings being close at hand; unlike the miles-wide stretches of the Brazilian Amazon where finally the mouth enters the Atlantic 100 miles (160km) wide. The eight-day journey from the highland cloud forest of San Juan del Oro near Lake Titicaca to Puerto Maldonado is one of the most spectacular boat trips in the world. One passes through white-water rapids, the pebbled beaches seen here on the Upper Tambopata, a macaw *colpa* and finally the sandy beaches and red cliffs of typical Amazon rainforest.

At the confluence of the Heath and Madre de Dios rivers on the frontier between Peru and Bolivia, a typically intense Amazonian sunset is reflected in the deceptively calm surface of the water (above left). The amount of moisture in the air adds to the depth of colours seen on most evenings.

At the end of a long day's boat ride, stopping to view wildlife at regular intervals, the full moon appears over the Manu river on the approach to the park guard station (above right).

Llamas, peaks and a mountain stream depict the origins and aspirations of the owner of this jungle restaurant (top left). A riverside shack with two tables, it supplies passing gold-panners with eggs and rice and occasionally a scrawny chicken is boiled into a weak soup. Over 90 per cent of the inhabitants of Madre de Dios are from the highlands; their knowledge of the forest beyond is slim and unlikely to grow.

Prospectors in the gold-rush town of Puerto Maldonado (bottom left). In the 1980s, when this shot was taken, any tourist visiting the city was described as 'hell bent on doing the Amazon the hard way' by the *South American Handbook*. The gold boom has passed but the dirt roads are now paved and daily flights from Cuzco bring eco-tourists on their way to rainforest lodges like Explorer's Inn, three hours up the Tambopata river.

A mackerel sky over the Pampas del Heath grasslands before sunset (right). This scene is particularly poignant for me, as I had recently been lost for 36 hours, with little hope of rescue. Cadbury's chocolate and this sky were my welcome back to the remote expedition.

At Huepetwe (below), between Cuzco and Puerto Maldonado, uncontrolled extraction of gold has created one of the worst environmental disasters in Amazonia. Over 25 miles (40km) of jungle floor has been dug up, filtered and sluiced using pure mercury to separate the precious flakes. The local rivers are bright orange with the run-off, and fish either die of the poison or transfer it into the food chain. The town spread amorphously in a lawless manner reminiscent of the nineteenth-century American West. Bars, brothels and a bank were the sum of commerce, and drunken gunfights broke out at weekends when the gold was sold. Sitting in a riverbed of its own creation, large parts of the town are washed away in the annual rains. The fall in the price of gold, and the exhaustion of 15 years' extraction, have meant that many people have moved on. Families, restaurants, schools and electricity have entered and soon it is to have a municipality, police, the vote and taxes.

A satellite town called Nueva (New) is a testament to the enduring strength of the human spirit. Built away from the frontline destruction, children bring an innocence to its ramshackle unnamed streets, their noisy games of hoopla, marbles and hopscotch and their home-made kites signifying normality on a bizarre stage (left and right).

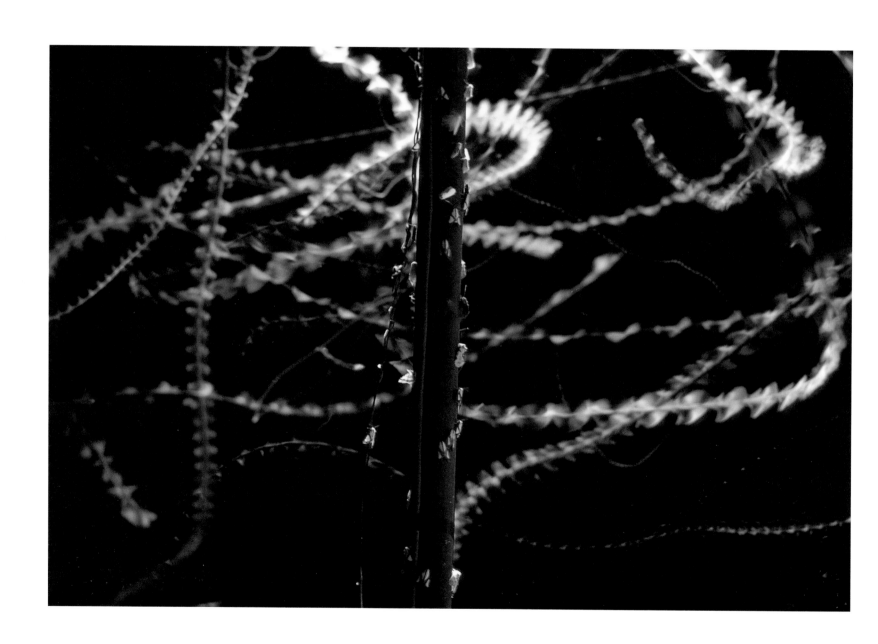

At night the two money-generating industries of mining and eco-tourism are obvious in their distinct styles. At the exit from Huepetwe spilled fuel and tin cans reflect the electric light of streetlamps and brakelights (bottom right), while in an exclusive jungle lodge, a mosquito-netted bed glows by candlelight as the full moon silhouettes the surrounding forest canopy (top right).

Moths gather and rest on the post of a streetlamp (left). Five seconds of time show their flight patterns in the night air. Bulb and candle alike lure them to a false moon and a hot death.

A research student prepares seeds and leaves for some flashlit photography (left). The guides at Explorer's Inn are usually biologists involved in coursework, explaining the ecosystems and wildlife to visitors in exchange for bed and board. There is no electricity, and the candlelight adds greatly to the atmosphere as the nighttime chorus of frogs and insects surrounds the stilt-supported, palm-thatched bungalows.

A wake for a baby girl (right). The anaemia that killed her was inherited from her mother, as was her compulsion to eat earth. The blanket is typical of highland weaving and is as alien to the forest as her family. Colorado is a remote satellite village that has grown around a gold-panners' camp on the banks of the Madre de Dios river. Slash and burn agriculture and flecks of gold barely keep body and soul together.

The future of Amazonia will be decided in this boy's lifetime (below). A Piro, in tree-bark *cushma* robe, his ambition is to fire an arrow as far and straight as his father. In 15 years' time he will have children of his own and choices will be harder and more immediate; in 50 years it is thought that little of the rainforest will remain, with vast tracts already owned by Japanese pulping consortia.

Esse Eja children in the Tambopata village of Infierno, 'Hell' (right). Colonel Fawcett, the famously disappeared explorer, described a friendly encounter with this tribe in the 1920s, referring to them as the 'fierce Guarayo'. Until 1997 their only contact with the outside world was conducted by boat. A new road has brought telephone, television and Teletubbies. Puerto Maldonado is now 40 minutes away by truck and an internet café on the main square can take people anywhere in the known universe.

Within the depths of Manu National Park live at least two uncontacted tribes. Living a stone-age existence of hunting and gathering, they are known through the stories of acculturated tribes like the Machiguenga, Piro and recently contacted Yora Yaminahua. In 1994 this arrow (far right) was fired at a passing boat and a tour group encountered a green-painted native standing alongside a trail. It is thought a small group of Amahuacas or Mashco Piro had made a rare visit to this part of the forest, but they vanished and were not seen again. After the brutality and disease of the rubber slavery at the turn of the twentieth century, these tribes prefer to remain hidden; their distrust of outsiders passed down through generations of oral history is all that guarantees their survival.

233

BIBLIOGRAPHY

ALEGRIA, Ciro, *El Mundo es Ancho y Ajeno* (*Broad and Alien is the World*) (Farrar and Rinehart, New York, 1941)

ALLEN, Catherine J., *The Hold Life Has: Coca and Cultural Identity in an Andean Community* (Smithsonian Institution, Washington DC, 1988)

ARGUEDAS, José María, *Los Ríos Profundos* (*Deep Rivers*) (Editorial Losada, Buenos Aires, 1958)

ASCHER, Marcia and Robert, *Code of the Quipu. A Study in Media, Mathematics and Culture* (University of Michigan Press, Ann Arbor, 1981)

BARTSCHI, André (photographer) and MACQUARRIE, Kim, *Manu: Peru's Amazonian Eden* (Francis O. Patthey & Hijos, Barcelona, 1992)

BATES, Henry Walter, *The Naturalist on the River Amazon* (London, 1863)

BAUER, Brian, *The Development of the Inca State* (University of Texas Press, Austin, 1992)

BAUER, Brian and DEARBORN, David, *Astronomy and Empire in the Ancient Andes* (University of Texas Press, Austin, 1995)

BINGHAM, Hiram, *Across South America* (Da Capo, New York, 1911)
—— *Lost City of the Incas* (Duell, Sloan and Pearce, New York, 1948)

CAMPBELL, Jonathan A. and LAMAR, William W., *The Venomous Reptiles of Latin America* (Comstock/Cornell University Press, Ithaca and London, 1989)

CARR, Archie, *The Windward Road* (Alfred A. Knopf, New York, 1956)

CASTNER, James L., *Amazon Insects* (Feline Press, Gainesville, 2000)

CIEZA DE LEON, Pedro de, *Descubrimiento y Conquista del Perú* (*The Discovery and Conquest of Peru*) trans. Alexandra and Noble Cook (Duke University Press, Durham NC and London, 1998)

COBO, Bernabé, *History of the Inca Empire*, trans. Roland Hamilton (University of Texas Press, Austin, 1979)
—— *Inca Religion and Customs*, trans. Roland Hamilton (University of Texas Press, Austin, 1990)

DAVIES, Nigel, *The Ancient Kingdoms of Peru* (Penguin, London, 1997)

EMMONS, Louise H., *Neotropical Rainforest Mammals* (University of Chicago Press, Chicago, 1990)

FAWCETT, Col. Percy H., *Exploration Fawcett* (Hutchinson, London, 1953)

FORSYTH, Adrian and MIYATA, Ken, *Tropical Nature* (Charles Scribner's Sons/Macmillan, New York, 1984)

FROST, Peter, *Exploring Cuzco* (Nuevas Imágenes, Lima, 1979/2000)

GASPARINI, Graziano and MARGOLIES, Luise, *Arquitectura Inka* (*Inca Architecture*) (Indiana University Press, Bloomington, 1980)

GENTRY, Alwyn (ed.), *Four Neotropical Rainforests* (Yale University Press, New Haven and London, 1990)

GUEVARA, Ernesto, *The Motorcycle Diaries – A Journey Around South America* (Verso/Fourth Estate, London, 1995)

HEMMING, John, *The Conquest of the Incas* (Macmillan, London, 1970)
—— *The Search for El Dorado* (Michael Joseph, London, 1978)

HEMMING, John and RANNEY, Edward (photographer), *The Monuments of the Incas* (New York Graphic Society/Little, Brown, Boston, 1982)

HENMAN, Anthony, *Mama Coca* (Hassle Free Press, London, 1978)

HUAMAN POMA DE AYALA, Felipe, *Nueva Corónica y Buen Gobierno* (Institut d'Ethnologie, Paris, 1936)

KEATINGE, Richard (ed.), *Peruvian Prehistory* (Cambridge University Press, Cambridge, 1988)

KENDALL, Ann, *Everyday Life of the Incas* (Batsford/G.P. Putnam's Sons, London/New York, 1973)

LAMB, F. Bruce, *Wizard of the Upper Amazon* (Houghton Mifflin, Boston, 1971)

LEE, Vincent R., *Forgotten Vilcabamba* (Sixpac Manco Publications, Wilson, 2000)

LEIGH FERMOR, Patrick, *Three Letters from the Andes* (John Murray, London, 1983)

McEWEN, Gordon and ISBELL, William, *Huari Administrative Structure* (Dumbarton Oaks, Washington DC, 1991)

MATTHIESSEN, Peter, *The Cloud Forest* (Viking Press, New York, 1961)
—— *At Play in the Fields of the Lord* (Random House, New York, 1965)

MORRISON, Tony, *Pathways to the Gods* (Michael Russell/Book Club Associates, London, 1979)

MORTIMER, William Golden, *History of Coca* (J. H. Vail & Co, New York, 1901)

MURPHY, Dervla, *Eight Feet in the Andes* (John Murray, London, 1983)

MYERS, Norman, *The Primary Source* (W. W. Norton, London and New York, 1984)

NERUDA, Pablo, *The Heights of Machu Picchu* (Librería Neira, Santiago, 1945)

PARRIS, Matthew, *Inca Kola* (Phoenix Press, London, 1993)

PROTZEN, Jean Pierre, *Inca Architecture and Construction at Ollantaytambo* (Oxford University Press, New York, 1993)

REINHARD, Johan, *Machu Picchu. The Sacred Centre* (Nuevas Imágenes, Lima, 1991)

ROWE, John Howland, *Inca Culture at the Time of the Spanish Conquest* (*Handbook of South American Indians*) (Smithsonian Institution, Washington DC, 1946)

SHOUMATOFF, Alex, *The Rivers Amazon* (Sierra Club Books, San Francisco, 1978)

SIMPSON, Joe, *Touching the Void* (Jonathan Cape, London, 1988)

SQUIER, E. George, *Peru, Incidents of Travel and Exploration in the Land of the Incas* (Peabody Museum, New Haven, 1877)

STAP, Don, *A Parrot Without a Name* (University of Texas Press, Austin, 1991)

STONE, Roger D., *Dreams of Amazonia* (Viking Penguin, New York, 1985)

TARDIEU, Jean Pierre, *El Negro en el Cusco* (Universidad Católica del Perú, Lima, 1998)

URTON, Gary, *At the Crossroads of the Earth and the Sky* (University of Texas Press, Austin, 1981)

VON HAGEN, Adriana and MORRIS, Craig, *The Cities of the Ancient Andes* (Thames and Hudson, London, 1998)

WILDER, Thornton, *The Bridge of San Luis Rey* (Longmans/Penguin, London and New York, 1927)

WISE, Mary Ruth and KENSINGER, Kenneth, *South American Indian Languages*, ed. Klein and Stark (University of Texas Press, Austin, 1985)

WRIGHT, Ronald, *Cut Stones and Crossroads* (Viking Penguin, New York, 1984)
—— *Stolen Continents* (Houghton Mifflin, London and New York, 1992)

ZUIDEMA, R. Tom, *The Ceque System of Cusco* (E.J. Brill, Leiden, 1964)

This bibliography, like the book itself, is aimed at the interested layman. For other works of reference, including the Colonial Chronicles, I refer you to the bibliographies of Hemming's *The Conquest of the Incas* and Wright's *Cut Stones and Crossroads*.

INDEX

Please note that **bold** page numbers refer to illustrated entries.

ACKNOWLEDGEMENTS

Each of the people named here has played their part in supporting me at some time over the past fifteen years. Some have known me all my adult life, others would say I haven't quite reached that stage yet. Though it is often a fantasy life, it is usually a lonely one. These people have helped get me through, and I thank them for their friendship and for the memories. To all those unnamed people with whom I trekked over snow, paddled round a rainforest lake or propped up a bar, I can only hope that I have done justice to your Peru as well.

IN CUZCO

Adolpho and Adela Arenas: Eric Arenas; Nick Asheshov and family; Constantino Aucca; Andre Bartschi; Javier "Pichicho" Bello; Richard Bielefeldt; the team of Bohic Ruz; Peter Bohm and Cecilia Vasquez; Guillermo Callurgos; the Carbajal family; Teo Allain Chambi; Danytza Contreras; Pepelucho and Susanah Corpancho; all members of Cotahuasi Expedition 2000; Paul Cripps; Tim Currie; Jean-Jacques Decoster; Kevin Doran; David Drew; David Espejo; Peter and Rosi Frost; Martha Giraldo; Boris Gomez; Tammy Gordon and her crew at Los Perros; Paolo Greer; Gunther Hane; Andreas and Rachel Holland and family; Quino Holland; Maxi Holland; Orlando James; Margo and Gladys Jimenez; Eirik and Heidi Johnson; "Gringo" Bill Kaiser; Cristina Orihuela de Lambarri; Juan Carlos Lambarri, Juani, Gabriella and Pablo Lambarri; Javier, Patricia and Isidro Lambarri; Jose Ignacio and Ana Maria Lambarri; Bella Lapa; Benoit de Lavaissierre; Pepe Lopez; Bruce McKenzie; Talo and Elisa Molinari; Don Montague; Gustavo and Mariana Moscoso; Franco Negri and Marlis Ferreyros; Mario and Sylvana Ortiz; Cecilia Pacheco, Douglas "Snake" Piquette; Ishmael Randall; Joaquin Randall and Jenny Moore; Johan Reinhard; Felipe Roa Obriola; Jorge "Cabezon" Sarria; Wolfgang Schuler; Pablo Segovia; Andy Sullivan; Reno Taini; all staff at Trotamundos where I wrote all the captions, all staff of Ukukus Internet Café; Bar and Disco; all at Centro Pi in San Blas; the Urubamba Posse; Orana Velarde; Barry and Charo Walker and all at The Cross Keys Pub; Wendy Weeks; Holly Wissler; Gary Ziegler and Amy Finger; Stefan Zumsteg.

IN LIMA

Carlos Aramburu; Cecilia Alonzo; Carmen Azurin; Amador and Adelina Ballumbrosio and family; Don Bandel; Marucha and Ana Teresa Benavides; April Borda and family; Giovanna Davila and Alejandra, Sebastian and Rodrigo; Alfredo and Talia Ferreyros; Georgie and Malu Fletcher; Inigo Garcia; Miki Gonzales; Alberto Grieve; Rosario Griffiths; Max Gunther; Rafo Leon; Oscar and Lorena Malca; Guillomar Pons and family; Mikko and Pia Pyhala; Cecilia Raffo; Adolfo and Sylvia Valle; Salvador Velarde and Carolina Vialle, Oscar Velarde, Ester Ventura; Jorge Vignati; Jorge Villacorta; Vanessa Villagran.

IN GREAT BRITAIN

Mariana Barreda; James and Jilly Bernard; Susi Boyd; Vanessa Buxton; Mary and Simon Campbell; Steve and Fliff Carr; Jason de Carteret; Colin Clark; Andrew and Rub Clementson; Ashleigh Cooley; Hugh Corbett; Marcela Cuneo and Mauricio Bonnett, Caroline Dashwood; Stefan and Gail Dennis; Ian Dickens; David Drew; Dale Durfee; Detta Fane Trefusis; Neil and Vicky Fox; Stephen Fulford; Mike Gambier and family; Damian Gascoigne; Laura Godsal; Leela Gourdeau; Mark and Karen Hannaford; Sloan and Candida Hickman; Mark Holborn; Chris and Joanna Humphries; Charlie and Bonnet Jacoby; Kath James; Zoe Johnson; Jemma Jupp; Mick and Rossina Karn; Malclom and Cecilia Macgregor; Luchi Marshall, Dennis and Fatima McNell; Marten and Renate Mijnlieff; the entire Milligan family; Ceris Morris; Sheila Mundle and family; Paul Murphy; Simon Newson; Rachel Nicholson; Sam and Abigail North; Luke and Bund Piper; Johnny Lyne Pirkis; Danny Pope; Jamie and Tara Robertson; the entire Robertson family; Christopher Sainsbury; Henry Stott; Liza Tarbuck; Victoria Upton; the entire Waghorn family; John and Louie Warburton-Lee; Jennifer Wilham.

ON THE OTHER SIDE

Patrick Milligan; Robert Randall; Charo Salinas; Alex Robertson; Theodore "Ted" Parker; Lorenzo de Szyslo; Barbara D'Achille; James Dirks; Pablo Balarin; Santos Sanchez; Sarah Jones; Dr Alberto 'Flaco' Grana, Renzo Uccelli, McKee, Luigi Taverna, Mirtha Gunther

I would also like to thank the following individuals, companies and institutions for their generous support and continued interest; Sergio Purcell, Felipe Castro, Charo Tejada and Miguel Irurita of Lan Peru, Amanda Coote of Acuvue/Vistakon; John Forrest and John Hemming of the Anglo-Peruvian Society; Robert Robinson of Blacks Outdoors; Ken Sethi and Howard Lee of Genesis Digital Imaging; Barry and Charo Walker of Manu Expeditions; the staff of the Ministry of Foreign Affairs, Lima; Javier Lambarri of the National Institute of Culture (INC); Ian Dickens of Olympus Cameras; Annie and Biddy Hurlbut of Peruvian Connection; all staff 1985-2003 of the Peruvian Embassy in London; Max Gunther of Peruvian Safaris; Rosario Griffiths and Juan Stoessel of Casa Andina Hotels, Oscar Velarde and all at La Gloria – Lima's finest restaurant, Don Montague of South American Explorers; Adolfo Valle, my farming partner in the Sacred Valley, and April Borda, my distributor in Lima.

Finally the team who put the book together; John Hemming for his kind foreword. Lineke Haydock and Debbie Knight and all at Imago. Shirley Greenall and George Papa at Book Systems Plus. My 'Publishing Godfather'– Christopher Maclehose. John Sexton for sage advice. And Laura Godsal without whose support this edition would not exist. And finally, the three musketeers; my excellent former editor, Richard Atkinson; fabulous designer Isambard Thomas; and Jane Turnbull, agent and solid rock.

For further information about exhibitions lectures and events, please visit **www.maxmilligan.com**

SPONSORS

Lan Peru is the high quality airline of Peru. With comfortable and regular flights and efficient service, it is the first choice for air travel around the continent. A member of the One World Alliance it is a subsidiary of Lan Chile.

Telephone: 00 511 213 8200
Office: José Pardo 513, Miraflores, Lima 18
Web site: www.lanperu.com

Inagro Sur is a privately owned company, involved solely in the production and exportation of fresh produce from Peru, under the Blue Hill label.

It was founded in 1989, by a group of growers from Cañete, where its main farming base and packing plant are located,

Telephone: 00 511 446-6785
Office: Alfonso Cobián 179 Lima 04 Perú
Website: www.bluehill-produce.com
E-mail: oficina@inagrosur.com.pe

MANU EXPEDITIONS

Manu Expeditions were the pioneering eco-tour operator within Manu National Park. Since 1983, their highly trained naturalist guides have been giving visitors the experience of a lifetime, whether it be camping alongside the rivers, or in the rustic luxury of Manu Wildlife Centre. They also manage horse-supported mountain treks.

Post: PO Box 606, Cuzco, Peru
Telephone: 00 51 84 226671
Office: Av. Pardo 895, Cuzco, Peru
Website: www.manuexpeditions.com
E-mail: adventure@manuexpeditions.com

CASA ANDINA HOTELS
Know-how, experience, dedication. These are the guidelines for Casa Andina, a new hotel chain formed by Peruvian investors, who aim to give each and every one of our guests that special and unique feeling that only first-rate service, a hospitable and comfortable hotel can provide.

Our mission: To transmit a new way of living the magic of the Andean world.

Information:
Av. 28 de Julio 1038, Miraflores, Lima 18
Phone 00 511 446-8848
Fax 00 511 445-4775
E-mail: ventas@casa-andina.com
www.casa-andina.com

Destinations: Arequipa, Colca Valley, Cusco, Lima (Miraflores), Lake Titicaca, Machu Picchu, Nasca, Sacred Valley and Tambopata

THE OUTDOOR EXPERTS

Established in 1848, Blacks Outdoors is the leading specialist in footwear, clothing and equipment for physical activity travel.

Website: www.blacks.co.uk
E-mail: enquiries@blacks.co.uk

GENESIS
DIGITAL IMAGING

Genesis is a professional photographic, digital imaging and display graphic lab based in Fulham, South West London. We provide a friendly and efficient service from conventional film processing and printing to the latest in digital technology, including digital drum scans, photographic prints from digital files and large format display prints.

T: 0044 (0) 20 7731 2227
Website: www.genesis-digital.net
E-mail: info@genesis-digital.net
Address: Unit D2, The Depot, 2 Michael Road, Fulham, London SW6 2AD, U.K.

RESTAURANT

Set in an old colonial house in the centre of Miraflores, La Gloria is the one of the favourite meeting places for the discerning foodies of Lima. It began with a profoundly mediterranean character, but today after nine years of experimentation around its original roots, while keeping the aromas and subtleties it can be said to have developed a character all of its own.
The bar provides a comfortable welcome and is the perfect place to unwind before enjoying one of the most memorable gastronomic delights of the city

Information:
Calle Atahualpa 201, Miraflores, Lima
Phone 00 511 4455705
Fax 00 511 4466504